‖‖‖‖‖‖‖‖‖‖‖‖‖‖‖‖‖‖‖‖‖‖‖

⟨⟩ **SO-AWU-634**

Best Easy Day Hikes Series

Best Easy Day Hikes

Death Valley

National Park

Second Edition

Polly and Bill Cunningham

FALCONGUIDES

GUILFORD, CONNECTICUT
HELENA, MONTANA
AN IMPRINT OF GLOBE PEQUOT PRESS

To buy books in quantity for corporate use
or incentives, call **(800) 962–0973**
or e-mail **premiums@GlobePequot.com**.

FALCON GUIDES®

Copyright © 2000, 2011 by Morris Book Publishing, LLC

ALL RIGHTS RESERVED. No part of this book may be reproduced
or transmitted in any form by any means, electronic or mechanical,
including photocopying and recording, or by any information storage
and retrieval system, except as may be expressly permitted in writing
from the publisher. Requests for permission should be addressed to
Globe Pequot Press, Attn: Rights and Permissions Department, P.O.
Box 480, Guilford, CT 06437.

FalconGuides is an imprint of Globe Pequot Press.
Falcon, FalconGuides, and Outfit Your Mind are registered trademarks
of Morris Book Publishing, LLC.

Project editor: Gregory Hyman
Layout: Kevin Mak
Maps: Trailhead Graphics Inc. © Morris Book Publishing, LLC

TOPO! Explorer software and SuperQuad source maps courtesy of
National Geographic Maps. For information about TOPO! Explorer,
TOPO!, and Nat Geo Maps products, go to www.topo.com or www
.natgeomaps.com.

Library of Congress Cataloging-in-Publication Data is available on file.

ISBN 978-0-7627-6052-7

Printed in the United States of America

10 9 8 7 6 5 4 3 2 1

The authors and Globe Pequot Press assume no liability for accidents happen-
ing to, or injuries sustained by, readers who engage in the activities described
in this book.

To the thousands of citizens of California and elsewhere, past and present, who laid the groundwork for protection of much of the California desert, to those who helped secure passage of the landmark California Desert Protection Act, and to the dedicated park rangers and naturalists charged with stewardship of the national treasure that is Death Valley National Park.

Contents

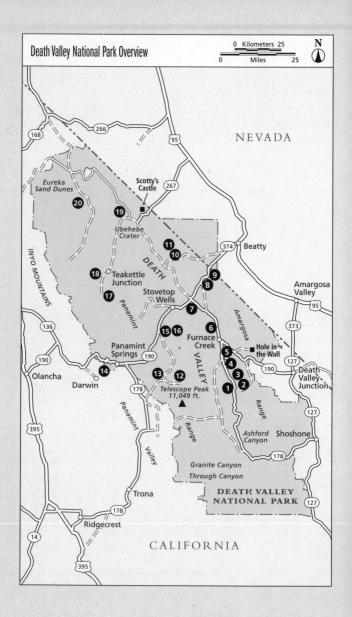

Death Valley National Park Overview

Introduction

Death Valley National Park contains some of the planet's most imposing and contrasting landscapes—from North America's hottest, driest, and lowest desert to soaring snow-capped peaks. With such extremes, Death Valley commands respect and entices discovery.

The California Desert Protection Act of 1994 upgraded and expanded the two-million-acre Death Valley National Monument into today's 3.4-million-acre national park, 91 percent of which is designated and managed as wilderness under the landmark 1964 Wilderness Act.

Despite its ominous name, Death Valley hosts more than 400 year-round and seasonal wildlife species. More than 300 of these species are birds, the great majority of which are seasonal migrants. Most wildlife is nocturnal and usually unseen by the human eye. Your day hikes in the park will reveal spectacular desert scenery, complex geology, primeval wilderness, historical and cultural sites, and perhaps even a fleeting glimpse of rare wildlife.

Best Easy Day Hikes Death Valley is a shortened and updated version of the Death Valley National Park section of *Hiking California's Desert Parks,* Second Edition. This compact guidebook features easily accessible hikes that appeal to the full spectrum of visitors—from kids to grandparents. These twenty hikes sample the best that Death Valley has to offer, for the casual hiker and also for those in search of a mellow start to a longer, more difficult hike.

Most of the hikes in *Best Easy Day Hikes Death Valley* are short—less than 4 miles round-trip and with less than 600 feet of elevation change. More than half the hikes are ideal for families with small children. All of the trailheads can be reached with a passenger car, and about one-third are accessed by a paved road. The best easy day hikes are well distributed throughout the more accessible central portion of the sprawling park, which is served by paved highways going north-to-south and east-to-west.

For the most part, options listed at the end of each hike description are extensions or longer variations of the hike. Consider these if you find yourself with that wonderful combination of additional time, energy, and determination.

Please keep in mind the park has very few developed trails. Wildrose Peak and Telescope Peak are the only backcountry trails maintained by the park. Most hiking is up canyons, across salt flats and alluvial fans, or over dunes where any trail would soon be erased by ever-shifting sands. Fortunately, hiking on these natural trails is often easier than on constructed paths.

There is a park entrance fee per vehicle valid for seven days. The interagency America the Beautiful and Golden Access passes are honored as well.

For current information on park regulations, weather, campgrounds, park resources, hiking trails, and road conditions, contact Death Valley National Park at (760) 786-3200 or visit the park Web site. The Web site for the park is www.nps.gov/deva/. You can check the official park Web site for weekly ranger programs, including ranger-guided walks offered during the peak season of November through April. You can also use the Web site to request a park map and brochure by sending an e-mail to the National Park Service Office of Public Affairs.

The Furnace Creek Visitor Center is open daily from 8 a.m. to 5 p.m. Ranger-guided hikes are offered during the peak season of November through April. Before you begin hiking, be sure to stop at the visitor center or a ranger station to get updated regulations and other information that will make your trip more enjoyable.

Death Valley is busiest from February through mid-April, and in November. Surprisingly, the lowest visitation occurs during December and January, not during the hot summer months as you might expect.

Wildflowers

Rain throughout winter and spring, along with warm, sunny days and lack of drying winds, produces good wild-flower years.

The park hosts more than 1,000 plant species, including twenty-three species endemic to the region as well as thirteen species of cactus. Desert annuals, like poppies and primroses, are the showiest.

Typical peak blooming periods are:

- Mid-February to mid-April at lower elevations (the valley floor and alluvial fans).
- Early April to early May for elevations between 3,000 feet and 5,000 feet (upper desert slopes, canyons, and higher valleys).
- Early May to mid-July for elevations above 5,000 feet (mountain slopes, pinyon pine/juniper woodlands).

Photography

The land of extremes that is Death Valley is best dramatized for the photographer when 11,049-foot Telescope Peak casts its afternoon shadow across the 282-feet-below-sea-level Badwater Basin. Combine this astounding vertical relief with recent volcanic craters, towering sand dunes, and flood-scoured canyons, and you'll see why knowledgeable photographers bring extra storage cards and batteries. These geologic wonders are most spectacular during the low-angle-light hours of morning and evening. Sunrises and sunsets are awe-inspiring.

Play It Safe

Wandering in the desert has a reputation of being a dangerous activity, thanks to both the Bible and Hollywood. Usually depicted as a wasteland, the desert evokes fear. With proper planning, however, desert hiking can be fun, exciting, and quite safe.

An enjoyable desert outing requires preparation. Beginning with this book, you need to be equipped with adequate knowledge about your hiking area. The potential hazards of desert hiking can be mitigated if you are prepared.

Dehydration

Plenty of water is necessary for desert hiking. Carry one gallon per person per day in unbreakable plastic screw-top containers, and pause often to drink it. Always carry water, even on short, easy hikes. As a general rule, plain water is a better thirst-quencher than any of the colored fluids on the market, which often generate greater thirst. Keep a gallon of water in your car so you have some available at the end of your outing, too.

Weather

Recorded temperatures range from a sizzling 134 degrees to a freezing low of 15 degrees. An annual average of less than 2 inches of rain falls in the valley. During some years no rainfall is recorded. Summer temperatures average well above 100 degrees. In general, temperatures will be 3 to 5 degrees cooler, along with increased precipitation, for every 1,000-foot vertical increase in elevation. For hiking comfort, the months of November to April are hard to beat. Average highs are in the 60- to 90-degree range on the valley floor, cooling considerably at higher elevations. The higher peaks and ridges are often snow covered from November to May.

The desert is well known for sudden changes in the weather. The temperature can change 50 degrees in less than an hour. Prepare yourself with extra food and clothing, rain and wind gear, and a flashlight.

Hypothermia/Hyperthermia

Abrupt chilling is as much a danger in the desert as heat stroke. Storms and/or nightfall can cause desert temperatures to plunge. Wear layers of clothes, adding or subtracting depending on conditions, to avoid overheating or chilling. At the other extreme, you need to protect yourself from sun and wind with proper clothing. The broad-brimmed hat is mandatory equipment for the desert traveler. Even in the cool days of winter, a delightful time in the desert, the sun's rays are intense. Don't forget the sunblock and lip sunscreen.

Vegetation

You'll quickly learn to avoid contact with certain desert plants. Catclaw, Spanish bayonet, and cacti are just a few of the botanical hazards. Carry tweezers to remove cactus spines and wear long pants if traveling in a brushy area.

Flash Floods

Desert washes and canyons can trap unwary visitors when rainstorms hit the desert. Keep a watchful eye on the sky. Check at a ranger station for regional weather conditions before embarking on your backcountry expedition. A storm anywhere upstream in the drainage can cause a sudden torrent in a lower canyon. Do not cross a flooded wash. Both the depth and the current can be deceiving. Wait for the flood to recede, which usually does not take long, before crossing.

Lightning

Be aware of lightning, especially during summer storms. Stay off ridges and peaks during storms. Shallow overhangs and gullies should also be avoided because electrical current often moves at ground level near a lightning strike.

Rattlesnakes, Scorpions, and Tarantulas

Unexpected human visitors easily terrify these desert "creepy crawlies," and they react predictably to being frightened. Do not sit or put your hands in dark places, especially during the warmer "snake-season" months.

Mine Hazards

Death Valley National Park contains numerous deserted mines. All of them should be considered hazardous. Stay away from all mines and mine structures. Many of these mines have not been secured or posted. Keep an eye on young or adventuresome members of your group.

Unstable Rocky Slopes

Desert canyons and mountainsides often consist of crumbly or fragmented rock. Use caution when climbing; however, the downward journey is usually the more hazardous.

Smooth rock faces such as those found in slickrock canyons are equally dangerous, especially when you've got sand on the soles of your boots. On those rare occasions when they are wet, these rocks are slicker than ice.

Zero Impact

The desert environment is fragile; damage lasts for decades—even centuries. Desert courtesy requires us to leave no evidence that we were ever there. This ethic means no graffiti or defoliation at one end of the spectrum, and no unnecessary footprints on delicate vegetation on the other. Desert vegetation grows very slowly. Its destruction leads to wind and water erosion and irreparable harm to the desert.

The Falcon Zero-Impact Principles:

- Leave with everything you brought with you.
- Leave no sign of your visit.
- Leave the landscape as you found it.

Avoid making new trails. If hiking cross-country, groups should follow one set of footprints. Try to make your route invisible. Darker crusty soil that crumbles easily indicates cryptogamic soils, which are a living blend of tightly bonded mosses, lichens, and bacteria. This dark crust prevents wind and water erosion and protects seeds that fall into the soil. Take special care to avoid stepping on this fragile layer.

Keep noise down. Desert wilderness means quiet and solitude, for animals and other human visitors.

Pack it in and pack it out. This ethic is truer in the desert than anywhere else. Desert winds spread debris, and desert air preserves it. Always carry a trash bag, both for your trash and for any that you encounter. If you must smoke, pick up your butts and bag them.

Remember, artifacts fifty years old or older are protected by federal law and must not be disturbed.

Treat human waste properly. Bury waste 4 inches deep and at least 200 feet from water sources and trails. Pack out toilet paper and feminine hygiene products; they do not decompose in the arid desert. Do not burn toilet paper; many wildfires have been started this way.

Respect wildlife. Living in the desert is hard enough for the wildlife without being harassed by human intruders. Please remember, this is the only home these animals have. Be respectful and use binoculars for long-distance viewing. Do not molest the rare desert water sources by playing or bathing in them.

Beyond these guidelines, refer to park regulations for specific rules governing backcountry use. Enjoy the beauty and solitude of the desert, and leave it as you found it for others to enjoy.

How to Use This Guide

To provide a geographic reference, Hikes 1 through 11 are numbered south to north and are located east of Death Valley in the eastern region of the park. Hikes 12 through 20, from south to north, are west and north of Death Valley in the western and northern sections of the park. The hikes presented in this book are rated according to difficulty, from easiest to most challenging. The "Ranking the Hikes" page will help you choose suitable hikes for everyone in your party.

Types of Hikes

Loop: A loop hike begins and ends at the same trailhead without duplication of all or most of the route. If there is any retracing of the route it is only for a short distance. Round-trip mileage is provided for loop hikes.

Out and back: Out-and-back hikes reach a specific destination and return via the same route. Round-trip mileage is provided for out-and-back hikes.

Shuttle: A shuttle hike is a point-to-point route requiring a car shuttle between the starting and ending trailheads. The mileage is the total distance between the two trailheads.

Use Trail: A use trail is an obvious footpath created by visitors that is not maintained by the park or another agency.

How to Get There

Primary access to the park from the east is NV 160 out of Las Vegas connecting with the Belle Vista Road out of Pahrump, Nevada, to CA 127. CA 190 heads west into the park from CA 127 at Death Valley Junction. From the south access is via CA 127 from I-15 at Baker. CA 178 leads west into the park from CA 127 near Shoshone. On the west side, CA 178 takes off from US 395 and enters the park by way of Panamint Valley. CA 190 takes off to the east from US 395 at Olancha, entering the park just west of Panamint Springs.

Maps

The map referred to as *Trails Illustrated Death Valley National Park Map* in the map section for each hike is the Death Valley National Park topographic map (1:160,000 scale), published by Trails Illustrated/National Geographic. It is an ideal overview map for trip planning and navigating the roads between trailheads.

In general, the more detailed 7.5-minute USGS quadrangle maps (1:24,000 scale) listed for each hike are not needed for hikes of less than 2 miles unless you are venturing beyond the described route. Refer to the small-scale hike maps provided in this book, especially for shorter interpretive trails that are typically well signed.

Campgrounds

To reserve a campsite in the Furnace Creek Campground, call (877) 444-6777 or go to www.recreation.gov. The rest of the campgrounds are first come, first served, and there is a fee for most of them. Check the current fee schedule on the park Web site.

Pets in the Park: Leave Home without Them

You can bring your pet to the park, but it isn't a good idea for you or your best friend. Pets must always be on a leash or confined in a vehicle. They may not be left unattended in a campground. You cannot hike with them on trails, cross-country, or anywhere else off an established road. You can walk with them on a leash on backcountry roads, but with the above limitations designed to protect park values, it is best to share other experiences with your pet, not Death Valley.

Ranking the Hikes

The following list ranks the hikes in this book from easiest to most challenging. The ranking applies only to the primary hike described, not to any options that may be included.

Easiest

Most Challenging

Trail Finder

Hikes for Canyons

Hikes for Open Desert

Hikes for Panoramic Views

Hikes for Historic Mines

Hikes for Birding

Legend

Transportation

=95= U.S. Highway

=190= State Highway

——— Park/Other Road

==== Unpaved Road

Trails

------- Featured Trail

------- Trail

→ Direction of Route

Water/Land Features

Body of Water

Dry Lake

Intermittent Creek

Waterfall

Spring

Sand

Symbols

12 Trailhead

■ Building/Point of Interest

P Parking

Restroom

Scenic View

? Visitor Center

Picnic Area

▲ Campground

▲ Mountain/Peak

× Spot Elevation

○ Towns and Cities

Land Management

National Park

East of Death Valley

1 Badwater

This is a perfectly flat hike on a boardwalk that leads you onto the salt flats at the hottest and lowest point in the United States and the lowest elevation you can drive to in the Western Hemisphere. This vast bed of salt lies 282 feet below sea level.

Distance: 1 mile out and back on boardwalk or 2 miles out and back to edge of the salt flats
Approximate hiking time: Less than 1 hour
Elevation change: Minimal
Difficulty: Easy
Trail surface: Boardwalk, clear salt flat

Best season: Late October through March
Maps: Trails Illustrated Death Valley National Park Map; USGS Badwater quad
Trailhead facilities: There is a signed parking area alongside a paved highway along with vault toilets and interpretive signs.

Finding the trailhead: The signed parking area for Badwater is on the west side of CA 178 (Badwater Road), 16.7 miles south of the CA 190/178 junction at the Furnace Creek Inn. GPS: N36 13.823'/ W116 46.273'

The Hike

As bleak as it looks, the popular hike onto the salt flats at Badwater is arguably the ultimate Death Valley experience. If you have been to Dante's View or Telescope Peak, you probably saw the human ants on the white expanse of valley floor and wondered what could be so fascinating. Here you will find individuals, especially families, cavorting like they're at the beach or enjoying a spring snow. To gain a genuine sense of the enormity of the salt flats, hike beyond the heavily traveled section.

The hike begins at the parking area beneath the cliffs that soar up to Dante's View, 5,755 feet above. There's a SEA LEVEL sign on the cliff face, high above Badwater, making very clear what minus 280 feet represents. Walk out to the salt flats on the causeway, but continue beyond the well-trod area, depending on the temperature and wind, to a clear area of the flats. Getting away from the highway is essential to get a sense of the magnitude of the salt flats. You'll reach the edge of the 5-mile-wide salt flats after only 0.5 mile.

Here, salt crystallizes when the groundwater that carries it to the earth's surface hastily evaporates. If you sit on the salt flats, you will find yourself among tiny salt pinnacles, a miniature mountainous world at the bottom of this mountainous basin. In close contact with the surface you will also discover that salt is a tough commodity. The white flooring of the flats is only inches thick, but very firm underfoot. Salt's power as an erosive force is noteworthy in this desert, where it functions much like frost heaves and ice do in a wet climate. Salt crystals grow and force apart boulders, breaking them down to be further eroded by wind and water. The salt crystal crust may be covered with a temporary lake following a rare heavy rainstorm.

Above the microworld of salt, the world of Death Valley soars. Less than 19 miles to the west is Telescope Peak (11,049 feet), the park's highest point. The difference in elevation between Badwater and Telescope Peak is one of the largest in the United States.

A hike at Badwater is an essential introduction to the expanse of the valley floor. The emigrants and the miners who lived in this environment were a tough lot.

The glare from the salt flats can be as intense as on snowfields at high elevation. Wear sunglasses. Do not hike

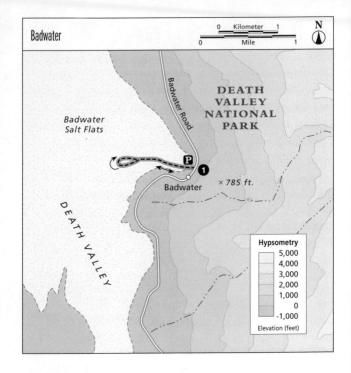

to the salt flats during the extreme heat of summer. Keep in mind that when the temperature tops 100 degrees F, ground temperatures exceed a sizzling 180 degrees F!

Miles and Directions

- **0.0** Depart from the trailhead.
- **0.5** Reach the end of the boardwalk at the edge of the salt flats. Continue hiking into the flats.
- **1.0** Turn around and retrace your steps toward the trailhead.
- **2.0** Arrive back at the trailhead from the salt flats hike.

2 Dante's View and Peak

This short, easy hike offers magnificent panoramic views of the highest and lowest points in the continental United States. Surrounded by some of the most dramatic and colorful relief found anywhere, you are nearly 6,000 feet directly above the lowest spot in the nation at Badwater.

Distance: 1 mile out and back
Approximate hiking time: Less than 1 hour
Elevation change: 229 feet
Difficulty: Easy
Trail surface: Clear trail
Best season: October through June
Maps: Trails Illustrated Death Valley National Park Map; USGS

Dante's View quad
Trailhead facilities: There is a large signed parking area with interpretive signs at the end of the paved road. The road climbs gradually, passing by an interim parking area just before the final ¼ mile, which has a grade of 14 percent.

Finding the trailhead: From CA 190, 11.9 miles southeast of the Furnace Creek Visitor Center and 18 miles west of Death Valley Junction, turn south on the signed Dante's View Road (paved, all-weather). Drive 13.3 miles on this steep, winding road to its end at the Dante's View parking area. GPS: N36 13.238'/W116 43.603'

The Hike

The unsigned trail to Dante's Peak is clearly visible to the north as it climbs toward Dante's Peak from the parking area. If possible, take this hike in the early morning with the sun at your back. This makes for better photography and for enhanced enjoyment of the superlative vistas and astounding 5,986-foot drop to the salt flats of Badwater, which sits 282 feet below sea level. The temperature at Dante's View averages 25 degrees cooler than that of Badwater. This exposed location is usually windy, necessitating a windbreak garment for the hike.

This lofty vantage point in the Black Mountains enables you to almost see, or at least visualize, how the mountains are both rising and slowly moving to the left (south) relative to the surrounding terrain. Looking across Death Valley to the highest point in the park, 11,049-foot Telescope Peak, you can easily note the major vegetative life zones stretching westward like a giant map. Bristlecone and limber pines thrive high in the Panamint Range. Below is the pinyon pine–juniper zone. Dante's View is situated in a hotter, drier midslope of blackbush and sage. Floods from the mountains result in graveled fans that support spreading root species such as creosote bush. Fresh water displaces salt from the fan edges, allowing mesquite to grow. Pickleweed gains a foothold in the brackish water below these edges. The muddy tans and grays of the valley floor grade into white beds of almost pure salt—a chemical desert.

From the parking lot, hike north along the road for 0.1 mile to where the Dante's Peak trail begins a fairly steep climb up the hill. Soon it winds to the left (west) and contours gently along the mountain's west slope. This route provides an even more impressive view down to Badwater, with an almost overwhelming vertical relief dropping more than a mile straight down! At 0.3 mile, the trail intersects the summit ridge, then climbs the short distance to the 5,704-foot-high point. Although unofficial, the trail is clear, well defined, and easy to follow. Return the way you came to complete this 1-mile out-and-back ridge walk, and don't forget your camera.

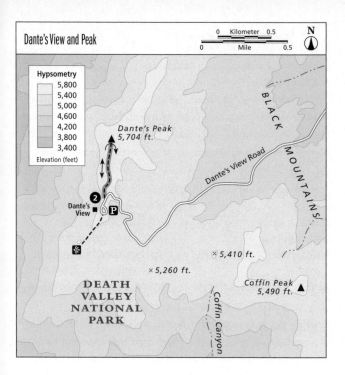

Dante's View and Peak

Option

For a slightly different perspective, hike a well-used path 0.25 mile southwest of the parking area. The rock outcropping at the point of the ridge is especially useful as a wind-break for setting up a tripod for early morning photography.

Miles and Directions

- **0.0** Depart from the trailhead.
- **0.3** The trail intersects the summit ridge.
- **0.5** Reach Dante's Peak (5,704 feet).
- **1.0** Arrive back at the trailhead.

3 Natural Bridge

A gently sloped canyon leads to a natural bridge that arches over the canyon bottom. The geological phenomena—faults, slip faulting, chutes and dryfall, natural arch formation—are explained at trailhead exhibits.

Distance: 2 miles out and back
Approximate hiking time: 1 to 2 hours
Elevation change: 520 feet
Difficulty: Easy
Trail surface: Sandy canyon bottom
Best season: October through April
Maps: Trails Illustrated Death Valley National Park Map; USGS Devil's Golf Course quad
Trailhead facilities: There is a large signed parking area with vault toilets and interpretive signs at the end of the dirt road.

Finding the trailhead: From the intersection of CA 190 and 178 in Furnace Creek, drive south on Badwater Road (CA 178) for 14.1 miles. Turn left (east) on the signed dirt road, and drive 1.5 miles to the Natural Bridge parking area. The road is washboardy and rough, but is suitable for standard two-wheel-drive vehicles. The trail begins behind the information kiosk. GPS: N36 16.921'/W116 46.069'

The Hike

Death Valley's fascinating geologic history is featured on the informational kiosk at the trailhead of the Natural Bridge hike. Bedding and slip faulting are explained on the board, so the canyon's convoluted display is even more impressive. Likewise, differential erosion is described and illustrated, preparing you for the bridge. Fault caves, the metamorphic

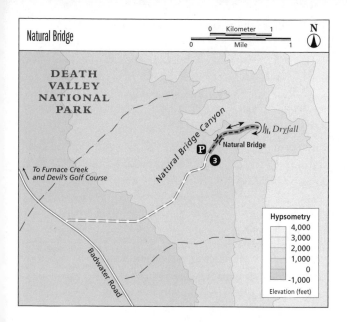

0   Kilometer   1

N

0   Mile   1

DEATH
VALLEY
NATIONAL
PARK

Natural Bridge Canyon

, Dryfall

Natural Bridge

P

3

To Furnace Creek
and Devil's Golf Course

Badwater Road

Hypsometry

| 4,000 |
| 3,000 |
| 2,000 |
| 1,000 |
| 0 |
| -1,000 |

Elevation (feet)

layers of the Artists Drive Formation, and mud drips are
other topics covered in this condensed, well-written version of physical geology. The kiosk is worth visiting before
embarking on this hike.

The canyon floor consists of loose gravel: that and its
sharp slope suggest a relatively young canyon. Death Valley's floor continues to subside while the Funeral Mountains
rise. Dynamic geologic forces are still active here.

The trail begins by passing through deeply eroded volcanic ash and pumice canyon walls. The gravel wash maintains
a steady 6-percent grade as the canyon gradually narrows. At
0.3 mile, the high bridge arches over the canyon bottom.
An ancient streambed is visible to the north of the bridge,
where floods swept around this more resistant section of

stratum before the pothole beneath it gave way to form the natural bridge.

Beyond the bridge, mud drips, slip faults, and fault caves appear, reinforcing the information you picked up at the kiosk. You can climb a dryfall at mile 0.8 with moderate effort, but a 20-foot dryfall blocks travel at 1 mile.

Retracing your steps down the canyon reveals even more examples of geology in action. Ever-shifting light creates iridescent colors. Traveling in the same direction as the powerful flash floods and the loads of scouring debris emphasizes the impact of water in this arid environment.

Miles and Directions

0.0   The trail leads northeast from parking area.

0.3   The natural bridge arcs over the trail.

0.8   Reach a small dryfall.

1.0   The canyon is blocked by a 20-foot dryfall.

2.0   Arrive back at the trailhead.

4 Desolation Canyon East

"Desolation Canyon East" is an unnamed but highly scenic canyon to the immediate east of the named Desolation Canyon shown on the map. It is a less crowded alternative to the nearby Golden Canyon. The longer version of this hike features moderate canyoneering to a high pass overlooking the Artists Drive Formation. Despite being only 5 miles south of Furnace Creek and close to Badwater Road, this deep, colorful canyon provides a feeling of solitude with broad vistas from the overlook.

Distance: 2 miles out and back to narrows; 4.2 miles out and back to overlook

Approximate hiking time: 2 to 3 hours

Elevation change: 250 feet to canyon narrows; 780 feet to overlook

Difficulty: Easy; moderately strenuous to overlook due to steep, unstable slope

Trail surface: Clear wash with three short rock pitches

Best season: Early November to mid-April

Maps: Trails Illustrated Death Valley National Park Map; USGS Furnace Creek quad

Trailhead facilities: A new loop parking area has been constructed 0.5 mile east of the Badwater Road.

Finding the trailhead: From the park visitor center at Furnace Creek, drive south 1 mile to the junction of CA 190 and 178 (at the Furnace Creek Inn). Turn right (south) onto CA 178 (Badwater Road), and drive 3.9 miles to the unsigned dirt road that takes off to the left (east). Drive 0.5 mile to the loop parking area. Desolation Canyon is the main wash to the immediate south from the parking area. "Desolation Canyon East" is unnamed and is the next main canyon to the immediate east of the named Desolation Canyon. The original road beyond the new parking area was washed out in August 2004 by a monumental flash flood. This 0.5-mile-long washed out portion of the road is now used as a trail to reach the mouth of "Desolation Canyon East." GPS: N36 23.728'/W116 50.345'

The Hike

This hike up the unnamed "Desolation Canyon East" is a highly scenic but less crowded alternative to the nearby Golden Canyon hike. An optional extended hike involves moderate canyoneering to a high pass overlooking the Artists Drive Formation. Despite its proximity to both the Badwater Road and Artists Drive, the narrow canyon provides a deep feeling of intimacy and solitude. The entire out-and-back trip provides a superb opportunity to observe the dynamics of badlands erosion, from mud-filled gullies to bizarre eroded shapes overlooking the canyon.

Because Desolation Canyon East involves a short hike at low elevation, the recommended time of day for the hike is mid- to late afternoon, when the cooler shadows fill the canyon. Upon return, in late afternoon to early evening, the brilliant light can be spectacular on the multicolored east-facing slopes above the canyon.

The main Desolation Canyon East is just over the low ridge to the north from the end of the old road, which is now used as a trail. Upon reaching the canyon in 0.6 mile, turn right (southeast) and head up the wide wash that climbs gently to the first canyon junction at 0.8 mile; stay to the right. Continue right at the next junction at 0.9 mile. At 1.0 mile, the canyon narrows with even narrower side draws. In places, the canyon is narrow enough that you can touch both sides at once. Retrace your route to complete this 2-mile round-trip to the canyon narrows.

Options

The hike can be extended to the head of the canyon or slightly beyond to an overlook. The next 0.1 mile reaches a couple of stair-step rocks that are easy to climb, before the canyon again widens. At 1.6 miles, what appears to be the main canyon to the left ends at a dry waterfall another 0.1 mile up. Continue up the narrowing canyon to the right; it ends at a steep, unstable rock chute at 2.0 miles. This is a good turnaround point.

If you've still got the urge and energy to explore, climb up to the right on loose, deep gravel to the overlook at 2.1 miles, which is at 840 feet in elevation. This relatively lofty vantage point provides a spectacular view of the varied colors of the Artists Drive Formation to the south. From this point, the Artists Drive is only about 0.3 mile west. Return by hiking back down Desolation Canyon East to complete this colorful 4.2-mile out-and-back badlands/canyon excursion.

Another enjoyable short hike is an out-and-back of about 1 mile up the named Desolation Canyon. The canyon mouth is directly south of the loop parking area. Desolation is another narrow canyon that weaves through colorful badlands. As you walk up take each right-hand fork to stay in the main canyon.

Miles and Directions

0.0 Depart from the trailhead at loop parking area.

0.6 Reach the intersection with the Desolation Canyon East wash; turn right up the canyon.

0.8 Where the canyon splits, stay right.

0.9 At the canyon junction, stay right up the main wash.

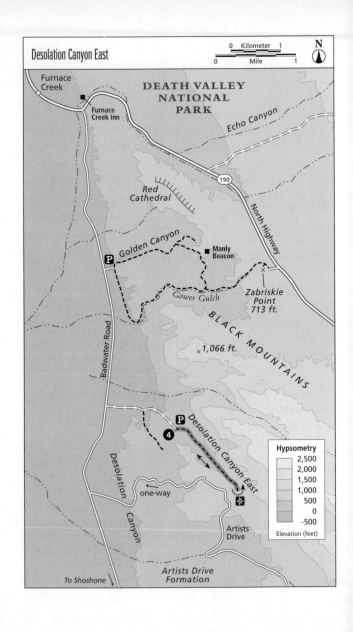

1.0 The canyon narrows.

2.0 Return to the trailhead via the same route.

Optional hike to overlook:

1.2 The canyon widens to a junction. Go right up the steeper, less-colorful canyon with more stair-step rocks.

1.6 At the canyon junction, stay right up a narrow gully.

2.0 The canyon reaches a steep chute. This is the turnaround point for the moderate hike.

2.1 Scramble up a very steep, unstable slope on the right to the overlook.

4.2 Return to the trailhead via the same route.

Optional hike up Desolation Canyon:

0.0 Depart from the trailhead at loop parking area.

0.5 Hike up canyon to the immediate south, staying to the right at each fork.

1.0 Return to the trailhead via the same route.

5 Golden Canyon Interpretive Trail/ Gower Gulch Loop

This fascinating journey through geologic time passes by rocks of different ages as the elevation increases, then loops back down to the floor of Death Valley past borax-mine tunnels. The first section is an educational geology nature trail. The scenery of the extended trip includes a colorful lakebed, exposed strata, and alluvial fan formations, along with spectacular scenery of the Panamint Range from below Zabriskie Point.

Distance: 2 miles out and back (6.5 miles for complete optional loop with side trips)

Approximate hiking time: 1 to 2 hours for short hike; 3 to 5 hours for longer loop

Elevation change: 250 feet (960 feet for the complete loop)

Difficulty: Easy (short hike); moderate (longer hike) due to distance and elevation gain

Trail surface: Sandy trail and rocky wash

Best season: November through April

Maps: Trails Illustrated Death Valley National Park Map; USGS Furnace Creek quad

Trailhead facilities: The signed trailhead and parking area, with vault toilet, bulletin board, and interpretive guide to the trail, is adjacent to the paved highway.

Finding the trailhead: From CA 190, 1.2 miles south of the Furnace Creek Visitor Center, head south on the paved Badwater Road (CA 178). After 2 miles, turn left (east) into the Golden Canyon parking area and trailhead, which is on the east side of the road. From the south, 2 miles north of the small town of Shoshone, turn west onto CA 178 and continue into the park. From Ashford Junction, go north on Badwater Road. The signed Golden Canyon parking area is

14.4 miles north of Badwater and can be seen just off the highway to the right (east). GPS: N36 25.246'/W116 50.795'

The Hike

Both the shorter and longer versions of this hike provide an incredible journey through geologic time, passing rocks of different ages as the elevation increases. An excellent interpretive trail guide to the Golden Canyon Trail is available for 50 cents at the Golden Canyon Trailhead. Ten stops in this geology guide are keyed to numbered posts along the trail.

Golden Canyon was once accessed by paved road. In February 1976, a four-day storm caused 2.3 inches of rain to fall on nearby Furnace Creek—one of the driest places on earth (where no rain fell during all of 1929 and 1953). Runoff from the torrential cloudburst undermined and washed out the pavement, so that today Golden Canyon is a wonderful place for hikers only. This pattern of drought and torrent follows countless periods of flash floods, shattering rockslides, and a wetter era when the alluvial fan was preceded by an ancient shallow sea. This is a land in constant flux.

At stop 2, it is easy to see how the canyon was carved out of an old alluvial fan made up of volcanic rock that predates Death Valley's origin some three million years ago. Layers in the rock tell the tales of periodic floods over the eons. Just above, the canyon displays tilted bands of rock, where faulting caused huge blocks of the earth's crust to slide past one another. The Furnace Creek formation is the compilation over time of lakebed sediments dating back about nine million years. The ripple marks of water lapping over the sandy lakebed hardened into stone as the climate warmed; the marks are evident on the tilted rock. Weathering and the effects of thermal water produced the splash of vivid colors seen today.

Mountain building to the west gradually produced a more arid climate, causing the lake to dry up. At the same time, the land was tilted by the widening and sinking of Death Valley and by the uplift of the Black Mountains. Dark lava from eruptions three to five million years ago slowed erosion, explaining why Manly Beacon juts so far above the surrounding badlands. These stark badlands rising above the canyon at mile 0.5 are the result of rapid runoff from storms on erodible, almost impermeable rocks.

Several narrow side canyons invite exploration on the way up Golden Canyon, particularly those opposite stop 2, and to the left and just above stops 6 and 7. The interpretive trail ends at stop 10, about 1 mile up the canyon at an elevation of 140 feet. For the short hike, this is your turnaround point.

Options

For a 0.8-mile round-trip hike to the base of the Red Cathedral, continue up the broken pavement. Hike past the old parking area to a narrow notch at 320 feet, directly below the cathedral's looming presence. Red Cathedral was once part of an active alluvial fan, outwashed from the Black Mountains to the south. The bright red color results from the weathering of iron to produce the rust of iron oxide. The cliff faces are made up of the more resistant red rock crowning softer yellow lake deposits.

Upon returning to stop 10 at mile 1.8, follow the signed trail to your left (east) up a steep gully well marked with trail posts. The trail climbs across badlands beneath the imposing sandstone jaw of Manly Beacon. At 2.3 miles, you reach a high ridge saddle below Manly Beacon at 440 feet. Follow the markers down a side gully to a wash/trail junction at 2.6 miles. The left-hand wash leads eastward up to Zabriskie Point. The right-hand wash/trail descends west to Gower Gulch.

If you walk up the main wash, you quickly come to the artificial cut made in the rock wall to divert Furnace Creek through Gower Gulch. This cut has sped up erosion in the gulch. Note the gray color of the rocks washed in from Furnace Creek, which lie on the bottom of the drainage in contrast to the reds and yellows of the badlands. Gower Gulch is largely the result of human construction to protect Furnace Creek from serious flooding.

For a short side trip toward Zabriskie Point, turn left (south) at the junction and follow the markers for about 0.5 mile to excellent views of Zabriskie Point, the surrounding badlands, Death Valley, and the distant Panamint Range. Zabriskie Point is another 0.7 mile and 200 feet above, and is accessible by road from the other side. It does indeed provide one of the most magnificent views in all of Death Valley, but its proximity to a paved road may detract from the hiking experience on the Golden-Gower loop. Thus, the overlook below Zabriskie Point is recommended as the turnaround point for a scenic side trip. Zabriskie Point is a popular starting point for those hiking 3 miles downhill through Gower Gulch, then across to the mouth of Golden Canyon.

Back at the trail junction at mile 3.6, there is no marker post to point the way toward Gower Gulch. Simply continue down the wash toward wide, gray Gower Gulch, which drops below mounds of golden badlands. At 3.9 miles, a side wash intersects the main wash; continue downward to the right. Early-day miners in search of borax have pocketed the walls of Gower Gulch with tunnels. These small openings are unsecured and potentially dangerous. A

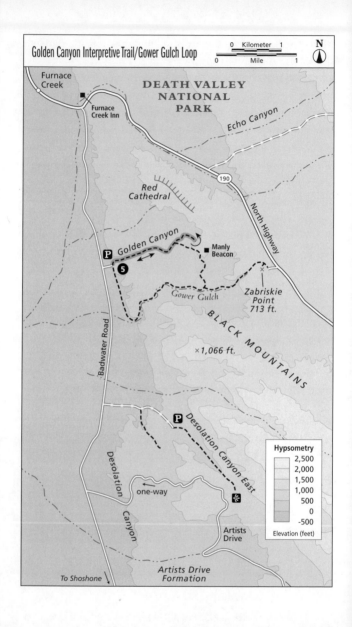

Golden Canyon Interpretive Trail/Gower Gulch Loop

0 Kilometer 1
0 Mile 1

N

Furnace Creek

DEATH VALLEY NATIONAL PARK

Furnace Creek Inn

Echo Canyon

190

Red Cathedral

Golden Canyon

Manly Beacon

North Highway

P

5

Gower Gulch

Zabriskie Point
713 ft.

Badwater Road

BLACK MOUNTAINS

×1,066 ft.

P

Desolation Canyon East

Desolation Canyon

one-way

Artists Drive

To Shoshone

Artists Drive Formation

Hypsometry
2,500
2,000
1,500
1,000
500
0
-500
Elevation (feet)

mile down, the wide gravel wash bends sharply left, narrowing dramatically with the bedding and faulting of red and green rock. The canyon floor then quickly drops 40 feet to below sea level.

At 5.2 miles, the wash meets a 30-foot dryfall. A good use trail curves around the rock face to the right. From here, the faint but easy-to-follow trail heads north 1.3 miles along the base of the mountains, paralleling the highway back to the Golden Canyon parking area, completing the loop and side trips.

Miles and Directions

0.0 Depart from the Golden Canyon trailhead (160 feet below sea level).

1.0 Reach the end of the interpretive trail at stop 10. Turn around and retrace your steps or continue for the complete optional loop.

2.0 Arrive back at the trailhead.

Optional intermediate points or complete loop:

1.8 Reach the intersection with the 0.8-mile side trip to the base of Red Cathedral. Backtrack to stop 10 and the beginning of the trail toward Manly Beacon.

2.3 The high point of the trail (440 feet) is below Manly Beacon.

2.6 Arrive at a trail/wash junction between Gower Gulch and Zabriskie Point.

3.6 Reach the overlook below Zabriskie Point (500 feet).

3.8 Backtrack to the trail/wash junction; begin to hike down Gower Gulch.

5.2 Reach the 30-foot dryfall in Gower Gulch; take the trail around to the right.

6.5 Complete the loop back at the Golden Canyon trailhead.

6 Harmony Borax Works

This short hike on a loop trail leads to a historic nineteenth-century industrial site on the valley floor. There are interpretive signs along the trail. The endless salt flats are an overwhelming sight.

Distance: 1-mile loop
Approximate hiking time: Less than 1 hour
Elevation change: Minimal
Difficulty: Easy
Trail surface: Asphalt walkway to Harmony Borax Works (wheelchair accessible); sandy trail to overlook and to salt flats
Best season: October through March

Maps: Trails Illustrated Death Valley National Park Map; USGS Furnace Creek West and Furnace Creek quads. The USGS quads that cover the route are not required for this hike; refer to the map in this book.
Trailhead facilities: The signed trailhead is close to the paved highway.

Finding the trailhead: The trailhead for the Harmony Borax Works Trail is 1.3 miles north of the park visitor center at Furnace Creek on CA 190. The 0.2-mile road on the left (west) is signed. The asphalt walkway leads west of the parking area. The optional 5-mile round-trip hike to the salt flats begins at the far side of Harmony Borax Works, heading west from the loop trail. GPS: N36 28.812'/W116 52.407'

The Hike

This desolate site was the scene of frenzied activity from 1883 to 1888—not in quest of gold, like so much mining activity, but of borax. Used in ceramics and glass as well as soap and detergent, borax was readily available here in Death Valley. Borax prices were mercurial due to soaring supply and moderate demand in the nineteenth century, so the industry was plagued by sharp boom and bust cycles. Here at the Harmony Works, the years of prosperity were typically brief.

Chinese laborers hauled the borate sludge in from the flats on sledges to the processing plant, the remains of which are the focal point of the hike. There, the borate was boiled down and hauled 165 miles across the desert to Mojave by the famed twenty-mule teams. One of the wagons that made this journey stands below the borax plant. Although the works were in operation only from October to June, working conditions for man and beast were harsh.

Although this is a short hike, be sure to bring plenty of water. It's a dehydrating experience.

Options
A 0.5-mile side hike to a low hilltop overlook gives you an excellent vista of the central valley floor. From here, it is easy to imagine the usual workday in operation at the Harmony Works. To the east of the hilltop is an area that appears to have been a dump for Furnace Creek. A rusty antique car rests on the hillside, surrounded by desert.

You can also reach Harmony Borax Works by way of a 1-mile-long bicycle path along CA 190 from Furnace Creek.

A longer optional hike to the salt flats—of about 5 miles round-trip—confirms the arduous nature of the work on the valley floor. An unsigned but well-trod path leads west from the end of the paved loop. It travels by a damp slough where groundwater percolates to the surface, causing borate

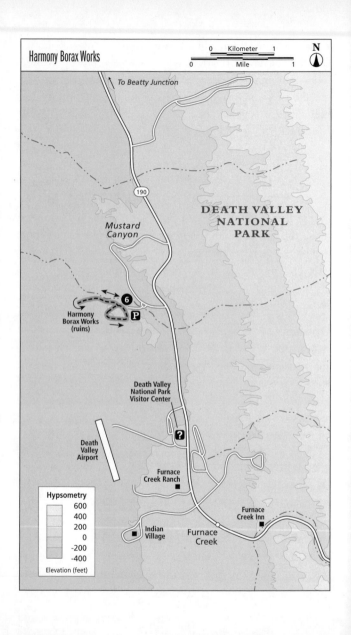

Harmony Borax Works

0 Kilometer 1
0 Mile 1

N

To Beatty Junction

190

Mustard Canyon

DEATH VALLEY
NATIONAL
PARK

6

P

Harmony
Borax Works
(ruins)

Death Valley
National Park
Visitor Center

?

Death
Valley
Airport

Furnace
Creek Ranch

Furnace
Creek Inn

Indian
Village

Furnace Creek

Hypsometry
600
400
200
0
-200
-400
Elevation (feet)

crystals to form. Farther out on the flats, mounds of borax mud remain where the laborers made piles to validate the works' mining claim more than a hundred years ago.

Miles and Directions

0.0   Depart from the Harmony Borax Works trailhead.

0.2   A trail leads south from the asphalt path to the hilltop.

0.5   Reach the outer end of loop; the use trail extends out into the salt flats.

1.0   Arrive back at the parking area.

7 Salt Creek Interpretive Trail

A nature trail on a boardwalk along Salt Creek features unique vegetation and wildlife, such as pickleweed, salt grass, and endemic Salt Creek pupfish found only here. There is an optional 5-mile hike north to Devil's Cornfield.

Distance: 0.5-mile lollipop loop
Approximate hiking time: Less than 1 hour
Elevation change: Minimal
Difficulty: Easy
Trail surface: Boardwalk; use trail to Devil's Cornfield
Best season: February through April
Maps: Trails Illustrated Death Valley National Park Map; USGS Beatty Junction quad
Trailhead facilities: The signed parking area with vault toilets and a signed interpretive trail are at the end of the road.

Finding the trailhead: From CA 190, at a point 2.4 miles northwest of Beatty Junction and 4 miles south of Sand Dune Junction, turn southwest on Salt Creek Road and drive 1.2 miles to the Salt Creek Interpretive Trail. From the park visitor center in Furnace Creek, drive north on CA 190 for 13.8 miles and turn left (southwest) on the signed road to the Salt Creek Interpretive Trail. GPS: N36 35.444'/ W116 59.442'

The Hike

Salt Creek Interpretive Trail is a fully accessible, lollipop-shaped boardwalk hike, with trailside signs providing interpretive information. The extended hike continues 4.5 miles up Salt Creek to the Devil's Cornfield on CA 190. There is a beachlike quality to the short hike, not only due to the boardwalk designed to protect this delicate habitat, but also due to the aroma of salt water, and the salt grass and pickleweed growing in dense clumps on the sandy stream banks.

The Salt Creek pupfish, endemic to Death Valley, are the stars of this hike. It's hard to believe these tiny relicts of the Ice Age can continue living in the hottest, driest place in the United States. In the spring, hundreds of pupfish swim in the riffles and pools of the creek. The fish are only visible February through May, with peak activity during March and early April. In other seasons they are either dormant (winter), or the stream is reduced to isolated pools (summer and fall).

The boardwalk runs alongside the creek and then crosses it in several spots—the first bridge is at 0.1 mile—so it provides an excellent vantage point to watch the pupfish in the clear shallow water or the deep pools. Pupfish are fast, small (not much longer than an inch), and enjoy zipping up and down the shallow riffles to bunch up in schools in the deeper terminal pools. As prehistoric Lake Manly dried up and grew saltier, these little fish were able to adapt to the new salty environment. Slimy green and brown algae, caddisflies, beetles, and water boatmen flourish here too, providing an adequate diet for the pupfish.

The walk out along Salt Creek is a startling change from the usual Death Valley desert floor hike. The sound of the merry running water in the winter and spring, with the flourishing growth of salt grasses, suggests a stroll on the beach. All that arc missing are the seagulls. With the interpretive signs along the trail, you can enjoy the fish and birds as well as learn about the dynamic changes of the desert habitat and the ability of some species to adapt to the harsh conditions.

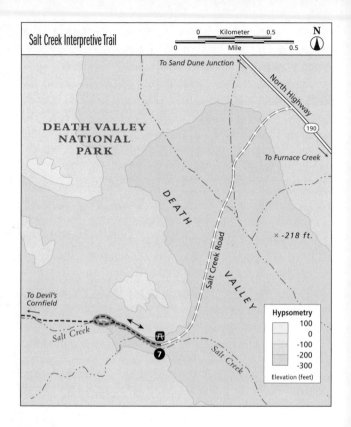

Salt Creek Interpretive Trail

DEATH VALLEY NATIONAL PARK

To Sand Dune Junction

North Highway

190

To Furnace Creek

× -218 ft.

Salt Creek Road

DEATH VALLEY

To Devil's Cornfield

Salt Creek

Salt Creek

7

Hypsometry

	100
	0
	-100
	-200
	-300

Elevation (feet)

Option

To leave the developed boardwalk trail, take the use trail from the far (west) end of the loop at 0.2 mile. The path heads north along the east side of Salt Creek. You can amble along the path, out and back, for as far as you want. You can take the use trail northwest for about 5 miles all the way to Devil's Cornfield, which is east of Stovepipe Wells Village adjacent to CA 190. Along the way you'll see more pupfish and a variety of birds. This is a good place to spot a great blue heron. Do not attempt this distance without an early morning start and a shuttle at the other end on CA 190.

Miles and Directions

0.0 The boardwalk begins west of the parking area.

0.1 Go straight to the first bridge for proper number sequence.

0.2 The use trail at the end of the loop leads 5 miles up Salt Creek toward Devil's Cornfield; continue on the boardwalk to return to the parking area.

0.5 Arrive at parking area.

8 Monarch Canyon/Mine

This out-and-back hike leads you down a rocky canyon in the Funeral Mountains to an 80-foot dryfall, a well-preserved historic stamp mill, and a desert spring with bird-watching opportunities.

Distance: 1.8 miles out and back from the end of Monarch Mine Road; 3 miles out and back from the Chloride City Road

Approximate hiking time: 2 to 3 hours

Elevation change: 310 feet from the end of Monarch Mine Road; 540 feet from the Chloride City Road

Difficulty: Easy

Trail surface: Four-wheel-drive road, rocky trail, clear wash

Best season: October through April

Maps: Trails Illustrated Death Valley National Park Map; USGS Chloride City quad

Trailhead facilities: Park alongside an unsigned road junction, or at the end of the dirt road. There is no established parking area.

Finding the trailhead: From Daylight Pass Road 3.4 miles east of Hell's Gate Junction in Boundary Canyon and 15.8 miles southwest of Beatty, Nevada, look for a road to the south marked only with a small sign recommending four-wheel drive. Carefully driven high-clearance two-wheel-drive vehicles can negotiate this road for 2.2 miles to the bottom of upper Monarch Canyon. High-clearance four-wheel drive is required for vehicular travel beyond this point to Chloride City. The rough Monarch Mine Road takes off south from this point. This road junction can serve as the trailhead for the hike down Monarch Canyon. However, you can shorten the hike by 1.2 miles if you drive down Monarch Mine Road to a point just above the dryfall; four-wheel drive is required. GPS: N36 44.216'/W116 54.736'

The Hike

You can start at the unsigned junction between the rough Chloride City Road and four-wheel-drive Monarch Mine Road (3 miles round-trip to Monarch Spring) or at the end of the Monarch Mine Road (1.8 miles round-trip). From the Chloride City Road junction, the trip starts out in rounded, low-lying hills. The four-wheel-drive road descends southwesterly, entering a rocky canyon after 0.3 mile.

At 0.6 mile, the road ends above a striking 80-foot dryfall. A major side canyon enters from the left, bounded by high cliffs marked by folded multicolored bands of rock. Continue left around the fall on the old mining trail. After another 0.1 mile, the trail drops to the wash, which is covered with horsetails and Mormon tea. This is favored habitat for quail and other birds. The base of the dryfall is definitely worth visiting, so turn right and walk 0.1 mile up to the precipice. In addition to the main wide falls, another smaller but equally high fall guards the canyon bowl to the left. The canyon walls are distinguished by shelf rock catch basins, overhangs, and contorted layers of colorful, twisted rock.

Proceeding down the sandy canyon wash, an eroded mining trail crosses to the right and then drops back to the canyon floor at 1.0 mile. Cairns are in place for the return trip. At 1.2 miles, you reach the wood and cement ruins of the Monarch Mine stamp mill on the left (southeast). The ore chute to the mill extends up an almost vertical rock face.

To further experience the rugged grandeur of Monarch Canyon, continue down the wash another 0.3 mile to the brushy bottom just below Monarch Spring. Here, the canyon bends sharply to the right and narrows. Hiking below

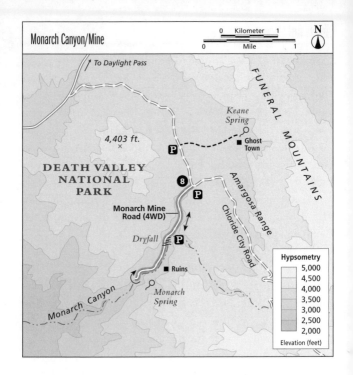

the spring would be difficult due to dense vegetation and loose, rocky side slopes. Retrace your route.

Note: A popular nearby hiking destination is the Keane Wonder Mine and Springs, located a few miles south of Monarch Canyon. At the time of this writing this entire area was closed to all visitor access due to mine safety hazards. The park is working to mine-safe Keane Wonder Mine and vicinity and anticipates reopening it to the public within two to three years. Check with the Furnace Creek Visitor Center for the current status.

Miles and Directions

0.0 Depart from the trailhead at the junction of the Chloride City Road and Monarch Mine Road in upper Monarch Canyon.

0.6 Reach Monarch Mine Road's end and an 80-foot dryfall.

0.7 The mining trail drops to the bottom of the canyon wash.

0.8 Walk up the wash to the base of the dryfalls.

1.2 Reach the Monarch Mine stamp mill ruins.

1.5 Arrive at Monarch Spring.

3.0 Return to trailhead on Chloride City Road by the same route.

9 Keane Spring

This easy hike to an old town site and spring offers broad vistas of Death Valley and the Tucki Mountains while traveling through gently graded foothills in the Funeral Mountains. Keane Spring is a microcosm of the boom and bust history of mining in Death Valley.

Distance: 1 mile out and back
Approximate hiking time: Less than 1 hour
Elevation change: 220 feet
Difficulty: Easy
Trail surface: Rocky, sandy road and sandy wash

Best season: October through April
Maps: Trails Illustrated Death Valley National Park Map; USGS Chloride City quad
Trailhead facilities: There is a parking area next to the barricaded dirt road at the trailhead.

Finding the trailhead: From the Daylight Pass Road 3.4 miles east of Hell's Gate Junction in Boundary Canyon and 15.8 miles southwest of Beatty, Nevada, look for a road on the south side that is marked only with a small sign recommending four-wheel drive. Turn south, and drive 2 miles to a barricaded road taking off to the left (east) to the Keane ghost town and spring. This former road serves as the trail. GPS: N36 44.421'/W116 54.820'

The Hike

The Keane Spring town site attests to the value of desert water. The town's brief existence (1906–1909) was based entirely on the availability of water here. When the Funeral Mountains were humming with mining activity during the rhyolite gold boom, Keane Spring promoters counted on providing the water necessary for both miners and ore processing. Ironically, the town was wiped out in a 1909 flash flood.

Why was the town nestled in the wash below the spring? In these rolling foothills of the Funeral Mountains, the open country features panoramic views of Death Valley and Tucki Mountain but also guarantees intense wind. The wash presumably offered protection from the latter. Apparently the town's opportunistic promoters ignored the dangers of flooding in the wash.

From the parking area, bear right and up on the faint trace of an old roadway toward a low ridge. At 0.3 mile, you will top out on the ridge. Continue northeast on an old road's path. Bright green willows mark the moisture of the spring in the depression ahead. Continue toward the greenery, heading downhill to the dry streambed. Follow the streambed to the dense foliage. The scattered remnants of the town of Keane Spring lie along the dry stream.

The only remains of the town are a few stone foundations left in tangled catclaw at 0.4 mile. Pieces of the old pipeline run from the spring to the southeast, in the direction of Chloride City, the primary water customer. Chloride City's brief period of prosperity was in 1906. The infamous San Francisco earthquake wiped out (economically) its investors, so Keane Spring was declining long before the flood arrived.

The spring's output has diminished since the beginning of this century. Now there is no visible flow—or even a gurgle of water—from the dense thicket of rushes and willows that jams the narrow spring, which is immediately above the Keane Spring town site at 0.5 mile. Birds and vegetation here demonstrate that enough subterranean

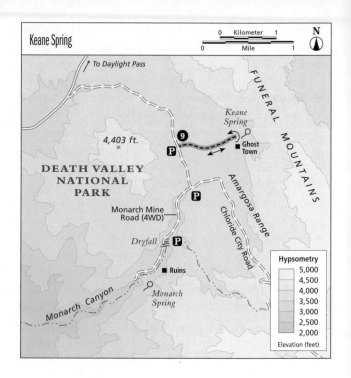

Keane Spring

0 — Kilometer — 1
0 — Mile — 1

N

To Daylight Pass

FUNERAL MOUNTAINS

Keane Spring

4,403 ft.
×

9

Ghost Town

DEATH VALLEY NATIONAL PARK

Amargosa Range

Monarch Mine Road (4WD)

Chloride City Road

Dryfall

Ruins

Monarch Canyon

Monarch Spring

Hypsometry

5,000
4,500
4,000
3,500
3,000
2,500
2,000

Elevation (feet)

moisture exists for nature to flourish. The coyote population is thriving also, judging from the droppings on the trail.

Keane Spring never was a very large town. With fewer than a dozen buildings and even fewer business establishments, its economic base was precariously thin. Nature has nearly erased its traces.

Note: A popular nearby hiking destination is the Keane Wonder Mine and Springs, located a few miles south of Keane Spring. At the time of this writing this entire area was closed to all visitor access due to mine safety hazards. The park is working to mine-safe Keane Wonder Mine and the vicinity and anticipates reopening it to the public within two to three years. Check with the Furnace Creek Visitor Center for the current status.

Miles and Directions

0.0 Depart from the trailhead.

0.3 Continue northeast on the ridgetop.

0.4 Look for the remnants of the town site.

0.5 Continue up the wash/trail to the spring.

1.0 Arrive back at the trailhead.

10 Titus Canyon Narrows

Titus Canyon contains the most popular backcountry road in the park. The rough four-wheel-drive road is also popular as a hiking route. And little wonder, for it has almost all of what Death Valley is famous for—rugged mountains, colorful rock formations, hanging gardens of rare plants, majestic cliffs, arched caverns, a ghost town, petroglyphs, wildlife, and a deep narrow canyon.

Distance: 4.2 miles out and back; 13 miles out and back to Klare Spring

Approximate hiking time: 2 to 3 hours for short hike

Elevation change: 650 feet; 2,100 feet to Klare Spring

Difficulty: Easy; moderately strenuous for longer hike due to distance and elevation gain

Trail surface: Rocky four-wheel-drive road

Best season: October through April

Maps: Trails Illustrated Death Valley National Park Map; USGS Fall Canyon quad

Trailhead facilities: The parking area with a vault toilet is alongside the dirt road.

Finding the trailhead: The two-way road to the mouth of Titus Canyon is 11.9 miles north of the junction of the Mud Canyon/Daylight Pass Road and CA 190, and 17.9 miles south of the Grapevine Ranger Station on Scotty's Castle Road. Take the signed dirt road east for 2.7 miles up the alluvial fan to the Titus Canyon mouth, where there is a parking area. Titus Canyon Road is one-way from the east, beginning at the canyon mouth. Embark on this hike early in the morning to reduce the chance of meeting vehicles; the 26-mile length of Titus Canyon Road means it is unlikely that vehicles will arrive in the lower section of the canyon before 10 a.m. GPS: N36 49.330'/W117 10.421'

The Hike

Titus Canyon is the longest and one of the grandest canyons in Death Valley. Morris Titus was a prospector who disappeared in the canyon in 1906 while searching for help after running out of water. Titus Canyon Road was built in 1926 to serve the town of Leadville, an investor scam that became a ghost town the following year. This 26-mile one-way unpaved road is accessible only by high-clearance vehicles.

Visiting majestic Titus Canyon by vehicle may not be the most satisfactory way to enjoy its scenery. By driving the 3-mile two-way portion at the western end of Titus Canyon Road, you can park and hike the dramatic narrows of the canyon. If you get an early start in the morning, you are less likely to encounter vehicles on the road. Driving to the canyon mouth also enables you to omit the alluvial fan hike, so common to canyon hiking in Death Valley.

Titus Canyon is a slot canyon, immediately narrow at its mouth. From the brightness of the desert floor you plunge into the canyon's cool shadows. Cliffs tower hundreds of feet above. Breezes rush down through the funnel of the canyon. The display of cliffs continues without intermission for 2 miles as you hike up the primitive canyon road. The variety of colors and textures on the canyon walls is immense and ever changing. The limestone layers are twisted and folded; fault lines run at all angles. In addition to the power of the earth's surface to rise and fall and shift, the power of water is visible throughout the slot canyon. The water-smoothed walls indicate the level of flooding. The curves of the canyon's path reveal the erosive power of the swift floods as they roar down the narrow opening with their load of scouring boulders. Flash floods are a real danger in Titus; often the road is closed for days after a storm in the area.

The 2-mile hike through the narrows is overpowering. Like walking down the nave of a European cathedral, hiking up (and later down) Titus is both a soaring experience, but also an immensely humbling one. The Titus Canyon Fault, which created the canyon, slices through the heart of the Grapevine Mountains, laying their innards bare for both the geologist and layman to enjoy. With the road as a walking surface, you can totally devote your attention to the details of this mountain cross-section, a rare occasion when hiking in Death Valley.

Option

For the longer hike, continue up the road another 4.4 miles to Klare Spring. The canyon floor is considerably broader, although quite steep, after you leave the Narrows at 2.1 miles, but the towering peaks of the Grapevines still provide a spectacular backdrop for the canyon hike. The spring is on the north side of the road at 6.5 miles. Springs are critical habitat for bighorn sheep, which gather nearby in hot summer months. Some marred petroglyphs are above the spring, a reminder that it is both unlawful and boorish to harm such artifacts. Return the way you came, enjoying your downhill trip, thereby completing a long 13-mile hike.

Miles and Directions

0.0 Follow the four-wheel-drive road east into Titus Canyon.

2.1 The narrow canyon opens into a broader valley; this is the turnaround for the short hike. Or continue on the optional hike to Klare Spring.

4.2 Arrive back at the trailhead.

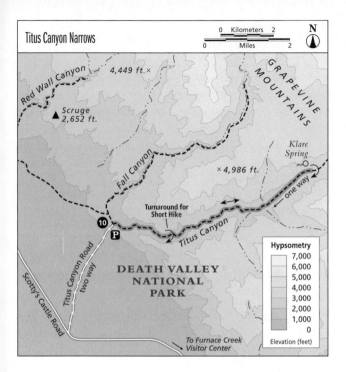

Titus Canyon Narrows

0 Kilometers 2
0 Miles 2

N

Red Wall Canyon

4,449 ft. ×

GRAPEVINE MOUNTAINS

▲ Scruge 2,652 ft.

Fall Canyon

Klare Spring

× 4,986 ft.

one way

Turnaround for Short Hike

10

P

Titus Canyon

Titus Canyon Road two way

Scotty's Castle Road

DEATH VALLEY NATIONAL PARK

To Furnace Creek Visitor Center

Hypsometry

7,000
6,000
5,000
4,000
3,000
2,000
1,000
0

Elevation (feet)

Option:

6.5 Klare Spring is on north side of road; petroglyphs are east of the spring. This is the turnaround for the long hike.

13.0 Arrive back at the trailhead.

11 Fall Canyon

This serpentine deep canyon in the colorful Grapevine Mountains features one of the deepest and most spectacular narrows in the park as well as habitat for bighorn sheep.

Distance: 6 miles out and back or up to 16 miles out and back for the optional out-and-back hike farther up Fall Canyon

Approximate hiking time: 4 to 5 hours

Elevation change: 1,300 feet

Difficulty: Moderate due to distance and terrain

Trail surface: Sandy path and cross-country on a clear wash

Best season: October through May

Maps: Trails Illustrated Death Valley National Park Map; USGS Fall Canyon quad

Trailhead facilities: There is a parking area with a vault toilet adjacent to the dirt road with a trail sign for Fall Canyon.

Finding the trailhead: The trailhead is at the mouth of Titus Canyon. The two-way road to the mouth of Titus Canyon takes off 11.9 miles north of the junction of the Mud Canyon/Daylight Pass Road and CA 190, and 17.9 miles south of the Grapevine Ranger Station on Scotty's Castle Road. Proceed northeast on the signed Titus Canyon dirt road for 2.7 miles up the alluvial fan to the canyon mouth, where there is a parking area. Follow the distinct but unsigned trail north of the parking area for 0.7 mile to an extensive wash leading up to the mouth of Fall Canyon. GPS: N36 49.330'/W117 10.421'

The Hike

Fall Canyon is a narrow, twisting chasm in the colorful Grapevine Mountains. Do not attempt this hike if wet weather appears likely. The canyon is highly susceptible to flash flooding. You could easily be trapped in one of the narrow stretches of the canyon by a raging torrent if caught during a mountain storm.

From the parking area at the mouth of Titus Canyon, hike north on an unsigned but easy-to-follow use trail, climbing gradually across several low ridges and gullies. At 0.5 mile the trail enters a side wash and then swings to the right (north) toward Fall Canyon. At 0.7 mile, the use trail tops out above the Fall Canyon wash, drops into the wide graveled wash, and vanishes after another 0.1 mile at the canyon mouth. Here, the canyon floor becomes your path.

At first the canyon is wide, up to 150 feet in places. At 1.3 miles the walls steepen and close in; dark shadows fill the bottom, adding to a feeling of intimacy. The canyon quickly opens to a huge amphitheater-alcove, bounded by sheer cliffs on the left (north), bending tightly to the right (southeast). At 1.5 miles, a large rock sits in a wide bottom that opens to colorful bands of red, white, and gray on the cliff faces. Continue left (east) up the main wash. The canyon narrows again at 1.8 miles, its sides pocketed with a myriad of ledges and small alcoves, only to open again with the west rim soaring 1,000 feet overhead.

At 2.0 miles, a narrow side canyon enters from the left (north) just above a massive boulder that blocks much of the wash. Continue to the right (northeast) up the main wash next to an isolated rock pinnacle.

Soon the canyon narrows once more, with rock overhangs reaching out above. At 2.2 miles, colorful folded rock dramatizes the powerful forces that continue to shape this rugged landscape. The canyon squeezes to a gap of only 8 feet at 2.6 miles, then widens, and then narrows again at 2.9 miles. A sheer 35-foot-high dryfall is reached at 3.0 miles.

The fall cannot be safely or easily climbed, so this is a good turnaround point for an exhilarating 6-mile round-trip exploration of Fall Canyon.

Options
If you want to continue up Fall Canyon, drop back down the wash less than 0.1 mile and look for cairns on the left (south) side (right side of the canyon going up). This bypass around the fall should only be attempted by those with at least moderate rock-climbing skills and experience. Begin by climbing a steep but solid rock pitch to a well-defined use trail that angles above and around the right side of the fall. Exercise caution on the loose gravel directly above the canyon. Immediately above and beyond the fall, the canyon becomes extremely narrow, bounded by sheer cliffs, folded layers of rock, overhangs, and semicircular bends of smooth gray rock. There are a few short rock pitches that can be easily scrambled up.

At 3.2 miles the tight chasm opens to more distant cliffs, but the actual wash remains narrow. At 3.4 miles, a massive boulder blocks most of the wash, with the easiest way around being to the left. Here, the hardest part about turning around is turning around; every steep-walled bend entices further exploration. The gray-walled canyon, polished smooth by the action of water, is left at 3.5 miles, when the valley opens to reddish rhyolite cliffs and peaks. At 4.1 miles, dramatic cliffs rise above steep slopes punctuated with jagged columns of dark rhyolite. You can follow the canyon up for another 3 or 4 miles but anywhere in this stretch provides a good turnaround point. Retrace your route to complete your exploration of this enchanting canyon.

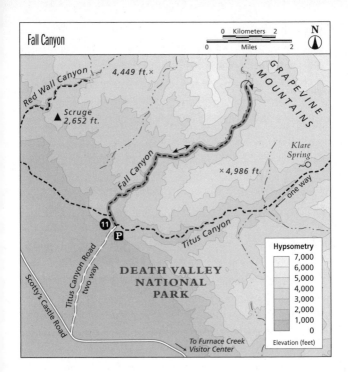

Fall Canyon

Miles and Directions

0.0 The trailhead is at the mouth of Titus Canyon.

0.7 The use trail meets the Fall Canyon wash.

0.8 Reach the mouth of Fall Canyon.

1.3 The canyon narrows.

2.9 Cairns mark a faint scrambling use trail to the right.

3.0 Arrive at the 35-foot dryfall.

6.0 Retrace route back to trailhead.

Optional hike:

3.1 The canyon narrows.

3.5 The canyon opens up to high peaks and ridges beyond.

4.1* Turn around anywhere and retrace your route back to the trailhead. (*At between 4.1 and 8.0 miles.)

8.2* Arrive back at the trailhead. (*At between 8.2 and 16.0 miles.)

West and North of Death Valley

12 Wildrose Trail

The Wildrose Trail takes you to a high Panamint saddle, and from there to the summit, from which the highest and lowest land in the lower forty-eight states can be seen. This is a cool alternative to the heat of lower elevations. Highlights include historic charcoal kilns, a rugged canyon, and scenic views of Death Valley.

Distance: 3.6 miles out and back to saddle; 8.4 miles out and back to peak

Approximate hiking time: 2 to 3 hours; 5 to 6 hours if climbing the peak

Elevation change: 740 feet to saddle; 2,100 feet to the summit of Wildrose Peak

Difficulty: Moderate; strenuous if climbing to the summit

Trail surface: Dirt path

Best season: September through mid-November; March through June (depending on snow levels)

Maps: Trails Illustrated Death Valley National Park Map; USGS Telescope Peak quad, plus the Wildrose Peak quad for those climbing the peak

Trailhead facilities: There is a signed trailhead with vault toilets at the north end of the Charcoal Kilns parking area.

Finding the trailhead: From CA 190 at Emigrant Junction, drive south on Emigrant Canyon Road for 20.9 miles to Wildrose Junction; continue east on Mahogany Flat Road (paved for 4.5 miles) and drive 7.1 miles to the Wildrose Charcoal Kilns parking area. In winter this road may be impassable; check with park authorities for weather and road conditions. The signed trail to Wildrose Peak begins at the north end of the kilns. GPS: N36 14.766'/W117 4.528'

The Hike

The Wildrose Trail is one of only two constructed trails in the park. It travels through classic pinyon pine–juniper forest to a high saddle, then zigzags to the broad, open summit of this central peak in the Panamint Range.

In spite of the impressive elevation gain to the peak, Wildrose Trail begins modestly. From the kilns at the trailhead, the trail charges 50 yards uphill to the northwest, gaining 60 feet, but then follows the contour of the hillside for the next mile. This section is a gentle warm-up for those climbing the peak. Along the route, rock outcroppings extend to the west, hovering over Wildrose Canyon below. This is classic mountain lion country.

Climbing only slightly, the trail joins an old logging trail coming up from the canyon. Numerous pine stumps are a reminder of the logging done here more than a century ago to supply the charcoal kilns during their brief use in the 1870s.

At the head of the canyon at 0.9 mile, the trail begins its climb. At 1.2 miles, the remains of a USGS water gauging station stand on the left (northwest) side of the trail. There is no longer any groundwater to measure. From the gauging station, the trail bends north and steepens sharply, gaining more than 600 feet in less than a mile. Rising to the first saddle at 1.8 miles, you have a magnificent view through the evergreens of Death Valley below. Unless climbing the peak, this is a good turnaround point.

Option

Wildrose Peak provides panoramic views of Death Valley and the surrounding mountain ranges. This broad, open summit in the central Panamint Range is reached via an 8.4-mile round-trip hike, with a vertical gain of 2,100 feet. Telescope Peak and Wildrose Peak are served by maintained trails and are the only hikes recommended during summer because of extreme heat at lower elevations. Parts of the Wildrose Trail may be icy and snow covered from November into April.

The trail climbs around three small rises before emerging on a ridge above the saddle below the peak. Here, at 3.1 miles and 8,230 feet, you can pause and view the 90-mile length of Death Valley. From the saddle, a mile of switchbacks leads to the summit. The trail snakes north, then south, then north, and so on, up the 800-foot climb. The changing direction enables you to enjoy a variety of vistas as you ascend the mountain, particularly as you near the windswept summit, which is clear of major vegetation. The meadowlike mountaintop is nearly always windy; appropriate clothing is a requirement, as are binoculars to enjoy the sweeping 360-degree view. Summer hikers will appreciate bug dope to combat flies and gnats.

A small rock wall on the peak was designed to give some protection from the wind. Or you can drop just a couple of feet down on the leeward side of the mountain to enjoy your stay and write a note for the peak registry. From Wildrose, you can see the vast area of mining activity in the north end of the Panamint Range. Just to the northeast, in the canyon below, there is a massive mining camp. Farther along Emigrant Canyon Road, mining roads crisscross the mountainsides. Rogers (with the microwave station) and Telescope Peaks loom above to the south. To the west is the mighty wall of the Sierras. To the east, across the valley, rise the Funeral and Black Mountains.

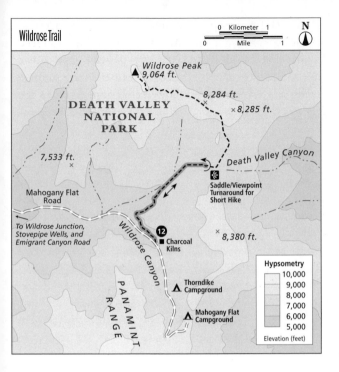

0 Kilometer 1

0 Mile 1

N

Wildrose Peak
▲ 9,064 ft.

8,284 ft.
×

× 8,285 ft.

**DEATH VALLEY
NATIONAL
PARK**

Death Valley Canyon

7,533 ft.
×

Saddle/Viewpoint
Turnaround for
Short Hike

Mahogany Flat
Road

To Wildrose Junction,
Stovepipe Wells, and
Emigrant Canyon Road

Wildrose Canyon

12
■ Charcoal
Kilns

× 8,380 ft.

P A N A M I N T   R A N G E

▲ Thorndike
Campground

▲ Mahogany Flat
Campground

Hypsometry	
	10,000
	9,000
	8,000
	7,000
	6,000
	5,000
Elevation (feet)	

The hike back down the mountain allows you to relax and focus on a new view of the scenery. Death Valley Canyon, extending eastward below the high saddle, is just one of the dramatic sights you may notice on the downward trip. Although this is a heavily used trail, its bending pathway preserves a feeling of solitude for the hiker.

Miles and Directions

0.0 Depart from the trailhead on north side of kilns.

0.9 Reach the head of Wildrose Canyon.

1.2 Pass the defunct water gauging station; trail bends and steepens.

1.8 Climb the saddle; views of Death Valley and Badwater open to the east. The trail turns north.

3.6 Return to trailhead on the Wildrose Trail.

Optional climb to Wildrose Peak:

2.9 Reach a second saddle with more panoramas.

4.1 Arrive on the south peak, the false summit.

4.2 On the north peak, the genuine summit, you will find a register in an ammo box.

8.4 Return to trailhead on the Wildrose Trail.

13   Nemo Canyon

The Nemo Canyon hike takes you on a gentle downhill traverse through open desert along a wide graveled wash, bounded by low ridges and multicolored badlands, providing a pleasing contrast to nearby mountain climbs. Several short, narrow side canyons branch out along the way.

Distance: 4-mile shuttle

Approximate hiking time: 3 to 4 hours

Elevation change: 1,450 feet

Difficulty: Moderate due to distance

Trail surface: Cross-country without a trail; open graveled wash

Best season: October to May

Maps: Trails Illustrated Death Valley National Park Map; USGS Emigrant Pass quad

Trailhead facilities: Park at the end of an unsigned gravel road at a paved T intersection. There is no established parking area.

Finding the trailhead: From Wildrose Junction (0.2 mile west of the Wildrose Campground), drive 2.2 miles north on the paved Emigrant Canyon Road. Turn left (northwest) onto an unsigned gravel road that takes off from the paved road as it veers right (northeast). Drive 0.7 mile to the end of the road at a paved T next to a gravel pit. A USGS benchmark is adjacent to this spot, which is the trailhead and jumping-off point for the hike. The end point is the broad mouth of Nemo Canyon on Wildrose Canyon Road, which is located down the canyon 3 miles southwest of Wildrose Junction and 1 mile southwest of the picnic area. GPS: N36 17.547'/W117 11.594'

The Hike

This down-canyon traverse begins in open desert country dotted with creosote brush and Mormon tea. Nemo Canyon

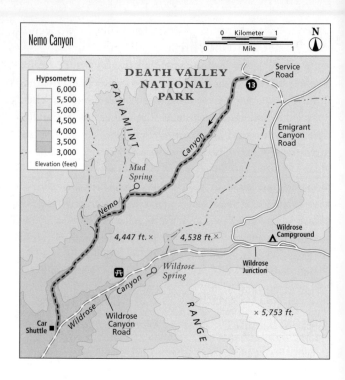

drops moderately to the southwest. To avoid walking toward the sun and into a stiff afternoon wind, make this a morning excursion if at all possible.

The canyon is wide open with low-lying hills and ridges—a pleasing contrast to nearby mountain climbs. Soon, a few scattered yucca begin to appear. At first the wash is braided and graveled but it becomes better defined, with a sandy bottom, after about 1 mile. At 1.5 miles the valley narrows a bit. After another 0.2 mile, red rhyolite bluffs rise on the left (south) side. Around the corner the valley opens in a semicircle, with several side canyons entering from the right (north). The white saline seep of Mud Spring is also to the right (north) at 2.0 miles.

At 2.2 miles, 100-foot-high cliffs rise on the left (south) as the canyon narrows slightly. After another 0.2 mile the wash parallels brightly colored badlands—red, white, black, gray, pink, and tan—with steep bluffs rising several hundred feet on the left. At 2.4 miles a huge valley enters from the right (north). At 3.2 miles, the canyon is marked by brown, deeply eroded conglomerate cliffs and spires. Large granite boulders appear, resting precariously atop spires of brown conglomerate. At times loose gravel impedes walking, but the steady downhill grade helps.

At 3.8 miles the canyon opens to the wide Wildrose Valley. In just another 0.2 mile, Nemo Canyon meets the rough Wildrose Canyon Road, thereby completing this point-to-point downhill traverse.

Miles and Directions

0.0 Start from the trailhead in Nemo Canyon wash.

2.0 Reach Mud Spring.

4.0 Finish the hike at Wildrose Canyon Road.

14 Lower Darwin Falls

Highlights of Darwin Falls include bird-watching along a year-round desert stream, with high multitiered waterfalls in a densely vegetated canyon gorge. The delightful moist microclimate of the falls is tucked away in a secluded canyon.

Distance: 1.8 miles out and back
Approximate hiking time: 1 to 2 hours
Elevation change: 350 feet
Difficulty: Easy
Trail surface: Dirt path
Best season: October through June

Maps: Trails Illustrated Death Valley National Park Map; USGS Darwin quad
Trailhead facilities: There is a signed trailhead parking area with a bulletin board at the end of the rough dirt road.

Finding the trailhead: From Panamint Springs, 29.6 miles southwest of Stovepipe Wells on CA 190, drive west for 1.1 miles to the signed Darwin Falls Road on the left. Turn left (southwest) on the dirt road, and drive 2.6 miles to the signed side road on the right (south) for Darwin Falls. You will notice a pipeline running along the road. The road is rough but passable for a standard passenger vehicle to the signed trailhead parking area. GPS: N36 19.686'/W117 30.870'

The Hike

Darwin Falls is nestled at the western edge of the expansion area of Death Valley National Park, adjacent to the 8,600-acre Darwin Falls Wilderness Area managed by the Bureau of Land Management immediately west of the park.

Darwin Stream is the only permanent water in this west-central region of the park. Flowing from the China Garden

Spring, Darwin supplies the Panamint Springs Resort with water via a pipeline visible on both the drive and the hike to the falls. This year-round water source sustains dense willow and cottonwood thickets in the valley and canyon, as well as a thriving bird population. Cliff swallows and red-tailed hawks soar overhead, and are among the more than eighty bird species that have been seen here. Brazen chuckwallas stare at intruders from their rocky lairs.

This hike is a radical change from the usual Death Valley outing. Right from the parking area, a streak of greenery and a glistening brook lead up the gently sloping valley floor. Hopping from one side of the stream to the other begins here, and continues throughout the hike. Steady footwork will prevent getting soaked, but you should exercise care on the smooth slippery boulders farther up the canyon. The Darwin Mountains, composed of black rhyolite, tower above the bright green grass, the willow saplings, the horsetails, and cattails.

At the notch of the canyon's mouth, another welded barricade remains. Because this is a public water supply, bathing and wading are prohibited. The high, dry trail is above the stream on the south side of the canyon.

There are many bends in the narrow canyon. With the steep canyon walls, as well as the willow and cottonwood thickets, this is a shady hike and an excellent outing for a hot, sunny day! A USGS gauging station on the north side of the stream at 0.7 mile, with its aluminum phone booth architecture, looks decidedly out of place in this Garden of Eden.

At 0.9 mile, you reach the falls, after hearing them in the distance. Double falls cascade over a 25-foot drop-off, surrounded by large old cottonwoods. Sword ferns, watercress,

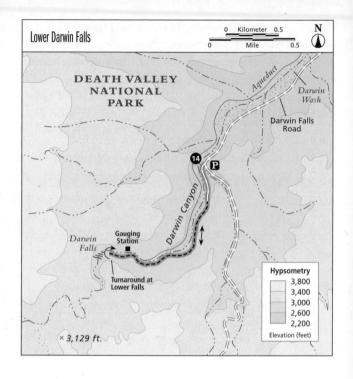

Lower Darwin Falls

0 Kilometer 0.5
0 Mile 0.5

N

DEATH VALLEY
NATIONAL
PARK

Aqueduct

Darwin
Wash

Darwin Falls
Road

14 P

Darwin Canyon

Darwin
Falls

Gauging
Station

Turnaround at
Lower Falls

× 3,129 ft.

Hypsometry

3,800
3,400
3,000
2,600
2,200

Elevation (feet)

and cattails flourish in the pool below. This is the recommended turnaround point. Hiking above the first waterfall is both difficult and dangerous. The park service has had to rescue visitors who were stranded on cliffs trying to reach the upper falls.

Emerging from Darwin Canyon is like an Alice-in-Wonderland experience. After you've been surrounded by humidity and greenery, the beige desert looks one-dimensional. The valley below the canyon is a striking transition zone, with the soft greenery of the stream ecosystem juxtaposed against the jagged dark rhyolite cliffs of the mountains to the south. The hike to Darwin Falls is a carnival of sensory perceptions. The smells, sounds, feel, and sights of this watery world make this an exceptional experience.

Miles and Directions

0.0   The trail follows the stream up the narrow valley floor.

0.5   Pass a vehicle barricade at the entrance to the canyon.

0.7   A USGS stream-gauging station is on the right bank.

0.9   Reach the lower falls.

1.8   Return to trailhead by same route.

15 Mosaic Canyon

Mosaic Canyon is a showcase of geologic wonder, so hiking into the canyon is like walking into a museum. Patterned walls of multicolored rock and water-sculpted formations await you in this picturesque northern Tucki Mountain canyon only 2 miles south of Stovepipe Wells.

Distance: 2.8 miles out and back to the lower dryfall; 4 miles out and back to the upper dryfall
Approximate hiking time: 2 to 3 hours
Elevation change: 600 feet to the lower dry fall; 920 feet to the upper dry fall
Difficulty: Easy to the lower dryfall; moderate to the upper dryfall

Trail surface: Dirt path with rock, then open canyon floor
Best season: October into April
Maps: Trails Illustrated Death Valley National Park Map; USGS Stovepipe Wells quad
Trailhead facilities: There is a parking area with a bulletin board at the end of a rough dirt road.

Finding the trailhead: Go 0.1 mile southwest of Stovepipe Wells Village on CA 190, then head south on the rough but passable Mosaic Canyon Road (signed). After 2.1 miles the road ends at the Mosaic Canyon parking area. The trail takes off immediately (south). GPS: N36 34.253'/W117 8.652'

The Hike

The fault in Tucki Mountain that produced Mosaic Canyon consists of mosaic breccia and smooth Noonday formation dolomite, formed in a seabed 750 to 900 million years ago. After being pressurized and baked at more than 1,000 degrees, then eroded, the resulting rock has startling contrasts of both texture and color.

Mosaic Canyon drains more than 4 square miles of the Tucki Range, so avoid it, like all canyons, in flash-flood conditions. Rushing water, carrying its load of scouring boulders, has created smooth marbleized waterways out of the otherwise lumpy breccia. Silky surfaces on the canyon floor gradually change to rugged lumps higher up its walls, reflecting the varying depths of floodwaters.

Like other canyons in Tucki Mountain, Mosaic Canyon is alternatively wide and narrow. The wider spots are more numerous and broad enough almost to qualify as inner valleys. Often hikers arrive at these open areas and turn back, figuring the canyon excitement has ended. With plenty of water and a broad-brimmed hat, you can continue exploring the depths of Mosaic Canyon. If it's a hot day, be aware this is not a deep shady canyon like those in the Grapevine and Funeral Mountains. This canyon offers little protection from the sun.

The first 0.2 mile of canyon features the polished marble surfaces that have made Mosaic Canyon a favorite destination of Death Valley visitors. After that, the canyon opens to a wide colorful amphitheater, swinging eastward to a broad valley with a 40-foot butte standing in the center. Use trails go in all directions, converging at the end of the valley where the canyon narrows again. To the right of the butte, a deep wash will eventually become a new branch of Mosaic Canyon.

At 1.0 mile, a small pile of boulders blocks a narrow spot. A well-traveled path to the left (east) provides an easy detour. After another wide spot, the canyon narrows again, where an abrupt 40-foot dryfall blocks your passage at 1.4

miles. The hike back down the canyon provides new views of Death Valley and the Cottonwood Mountains in the distance. Sliding down the short water chutes on the return to the trailhead increases the marbleized beauty of these breccia formations; generations of hikers have added to water's erosive force in creating these smooth rocks.

You can sometimes see bighorn sheep above Mosaic Canyon, so keep a watchful eye out for these reclusive desert denizens.

Option

It is possible to get around the dry fall on a well traveled, marked trail. Drop 50 yards back from the dry fall to the trail on the sloping canyon wall to the south. This path takes you to the upper region of Mosaic Canyon, where another 0.5 mile and 320 feet of elevation gain through marbleized chutes and narrows awaits you. A steep marble funnel, 50 feet high, halts the hike at about 2 miles. It's a striking spot, with eroding, fragmented Tucki Mountain rising above the silky smooth waterslide.

Miles and Directions

- **0.0** The trail begins in a wash from the parking area behind the information sign.
- **0.2** Enter the wide-open canyon.
- **1.4** A 40-foot dryfall blocks the canyon; 50 yards back, cairns and arrows mark the side trail for the longer option to the upper dryfall.
- **2.8** Arrive back at trailhead by following the canyon back down to the trailhead for the shorter hike.

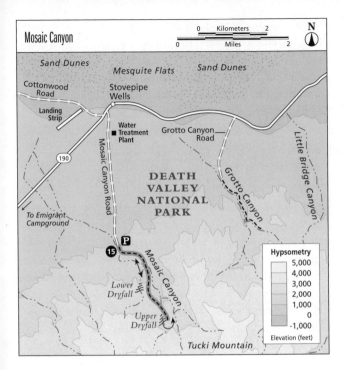

Option:

1.4 Take the side trail to the upper dryfall.

2.0 Upper dryfall blocks further passage. Turn around and retrace your steps to the trailhead.

4.0 Arrive at trailhead.

16 Grotto Canyon

This out-and-back Tucki Mountain canyon hike winds through water-carved grottos and narrows of polished rock to a high dryfall.

Distance: 4 miles out and back
Approximate hiking time: 2 to 3 hours
Elevation change: 800 feet
Difficulty: Easy
Trail surface: Sandy rocky wash, then open canyon floor
Best season: October through April
Maps: Trails Illustrated Death Valley National Park Map; USGS Grotto Canyon quad
Trailhead facilities: Park next to a turnaround at the end of the dirt road before reaching the Wilderness boundary sign.

Finding the trailhead: The Grotto Canyon access road heads south from CA 190, 2.4 miles east of Stovepipe Wells Village and 3.9 miles west of Sand Dunes Junction. The road is signed for Grotto Canyon and four-wheel-drive vehicles. The road ends for most vehicles after 1.1 miles south of CA 190, at which point the road changes to soft gravel above the wash. The road/trail continues up the wash to the canyon. GPS near the canyon mouth: N36 35.30'/W117 6.70'

The Hike

With careful driving, a passenger vehicle can negotiate the road to the wash of the Grotto Canyon hike. For the additional mile to the canyon entrance, the wash's soft gravel requires high clearance and four-wheel drive. A WILDERNESS/NO VEHICLES sign marks the end of the road. Conditions in this canyon change with each flood. At times the

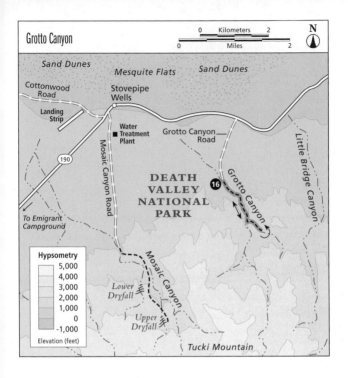

0   Kilometers   2

0   Miles   2

N

Sand Dunes

Mesquite Flats   Sand Dunes

Cottonwood
Road   Stovepipe
Wells

Landing
Strip

Water
■ Treatment
Plant   Grotto Canyon
Road

190

DEATH
VALLEY
NATIONAL
PARK

16

Grotto Canyon

Little Bridge Canyon

To Emigrant
Campground

Mosaic Canyon Road

Mosaic Canyon

Hypsometry

5,000
4,000
3,000
2,000
1,000
0
-1,000

Elevation (feet)

Lower
Dryfall

Upper
Dryfall

Tucki Mountain

gravel is deep and the dryfalls easy to scale, but often floods have scoured away the gravel, making exploration more of a challenge.

Like the other Tucki Mountain canyons, Grotto Canyon is very broad—up to 200 yards wide in many areas. Deeply eroded canyon walls stand like medieval castle ramparts, with short serpentine pathways in their lower reaches. The narrows at 1.8 miles bring welcome shade after the journey up the graveled canyon bottom. A pair of ravens nesting in the aerie alcove above the grotto may provide suitable visual and sound effects for the hiker approaching this almost cavelike section of the canyon. About 0.1 mile back down the canyon, a trail marked with cairns on the eastern side leads you around this barrier to the canyon above. Another dryfall at 2.0 miles will block your travels.

Even with its proximity to Stovepipe Wells, Grotto Canyon is not heavily visited. The adventuresome hiker can enjoy desert exploration and solitude without a lengthy drive. The intense silence above Mesquite Flat rings in your ears between cries of the ravens.

Hiking back to the road, the dunes stretch out below, framed by the Cottonwood and Grapevine Mountains. Grotto Canyon is a desert wonder of a smaller dimension.

Miles and Directions

0.0   Follow the gravel jeep road up the wash.

0.9   The canyon narrows.

1.8   Reach the first dryfall.

2.0   Arrive at the second dryfall.

4.0   Follow the canyon back down to the trailhead.

17 The Grandstand

The Grandstand is a high mound of dark rock contrasting dramatically within the gleaming white Racetrack Playa. A mountainous backdrop, intense isolation, and outstanding scenic views await the visitor.

Distance: 1 mile out and back
Approximate hiking time: Less than 1 hour
Elevation change: Minimal
Difficulty: Easy; strenuous to Ubehebe Peak
Trail surface: Smooth sand
Best season: October through April
Maps: Trails Illustrated Death Valley National Park Map; USGS Ubehebe Peak quad
Trailhead facilities: The parking area with an interpretive sign is adjacent to the dirt Racetrack Valley Road.

Finding the trailhead: From the junction of Scotty's Castle Road and Ubehebe Crater Road in the northeastern corner of the park, head northwest on the paved Ubehebe Crater Road. The pavement ends after 5.3 miles at the turnoff to Ubehebe Crater. Continue south on the washboard, dirt Racetrack Valley Road for 19.7 miles to Tea-kettle Junction. Take the right-hand turn for Racetrack Valley Road and drive another 5.7 miles to the Grandstand parking area, which is opposite the "grandstand" of gray rocks in the dry lakebed east of the road. GPS: N36 41.594'/W117 35.561'

The Hike

The Grandstand is about 0.5 mile directly east of the parking area. It consists of a large, 70-foot-high mound of gray rocks rising in stark contrast to the surrounding white flatness of the Racetrack Playa, a dry lakebed. For added perspective, walk around the Grandstand, then scramble up some of the large boulders. The Grandstand can be easily climbed 40 to 50 feet above the playa. Once in a while rocks fall from the Grandstand to the lakebed, and then they move! However, don't expect to see the famous "moving rocks" here as they are found a couple of miles to the south. The Grandstand provides a superb perspective of formidable 5,678-foot-high Ubehebe Peak, rising 2,000 feet 1.5 miles to the west.

Options

If time allows, drive south from the Grandstand another 2 miles. Look for a short use trail heading eastward across the southern end of the Racetrack Playa. This is where you will find the best view of the mysterious trails of the moving rocks. The mystery of these mobile rocks is heightened by the fact that no one has ever seen them move. Most likely the rocks are swept by powerful winds when the fine clay surface of the lakebed is made slick by heavy rain.

A far more difficult option is to hike up toward Ube-hebe Peak. The trail heads west of the Racetrack Valley Road from the Grandstand parking area. Be sure to carry sufficient water for this high, dry desert climb. The clear trail, originally an old mining path, begins by ascending gradually to the northwest up an alluvial fan clothed with desert trumpet and creosote bush. Within 0.5 mile, the trail begins a long series of steep switchbacks up the east face of the 5,519-foot north peak. This imposing buttress is made even more impressive by broken cliffs of desert varnish. After climbing nearly 1,200 feet in 1.8 miles the trail reaches the north ridge of the peak, which is just beyond an outcropping of limestone where the blue-green copper of malachite rock lines a shallow mine digging. From this point

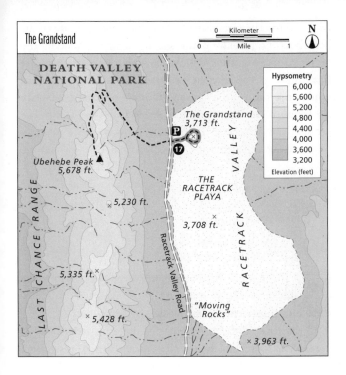

Hypsometry
6,000
5,600
5,200
4,800
4,400
4,000
3,600
3,200
Elevation (feet)

The Grandstand
3,713 ft.

DEATH VALLEY
NATIONAL PARK

Ubehebe Peak
5,678 ft.

THE
RACETRACK
PLAYA

× 5,230 ft.

× 3,708 ft.

RACETRACK

VALLEY

5,335 ft. ×

Racetrack Valley Road

LAST CHANCE RANGE

× 5,428 ft.

"Moving
Rocks"

× 3,963 ft.

0   Kilometer   1

0   Mile   1

N

a trail takes off to the right, ending after 0.1 mile at an overlook above an old mine entrance. The summit of Ubehebe
Peak can be seen in the distance beyond the north peak,
which rises directly above. This is a good turnaround point.

If you wish to continue, take the left-hand trail, which
climbs steeply up the ridge through the rocks to 5,160 feet
at 2.0 miles. The trail then wraps around the west side of
the mountain, reaching an elevation of 5,440 feet at 2.4
miles. From here on, the trail becomes rougher and more
faint, compensated somewhat by stupendous views of the
playa to the southeast. The trail then drops for 0.2 mile to

the 5,220-foot saddle between the two peaks. Any resemblance to a trail ends at the saddle, which is a good end point for those not wishing to scramble up the steep rocky ridge another 0.4 mile and 460 vertical feet to the top of Ubehebe Peak.

From the saddle, the Saline Valley lies 4,000 feet below to the west. Beyond is the soaring 10,000-foot crest of the Inyo Mountains, with the even higher Sierra Nevada looming farther to the west. Look for Mount Whitney. The crown of Death Valley—lofty Telescope Peak—can be seen to the southeast, along with the vast wooded plateau of Hunter Mountain. Perhaps most impressive is the eagle's-eye view of the gleaming white Racetrack Playa encircling the tiny dark specks of the Grandstand far below.

Miles and Directions

0.0   Head east from the Grandstand trailhead.

0.5   Reach the Grandstand.

1.0   Walk west across the playa back to the trailhead.

18 Ubehebe Lead Mine/ Corridor Canyon

This exploration of a historic early-twentieth-century mine site with a tram will appeal to history and mining buffs. The longer leg in Corridor Canyon will enchant those who appreciate scenic vistas of desert cliffs and mountains.

Distance: 1 mile out and back to mine; 5 to 10 miles out and back in canyon

Approximate hiking time: 1 to 2 hours to mine; 4 to 5 hours for the canyon, depending on the turnaround point

Elevation change: 380 feet to the mine overlook

Difficulty: Moderate for both hikes due to steep slope to mine and distance in canyon

Trail surface: Dirt path to mine; clear wash in canyon

Best season: October through March

Maps: Trails Illustrated Death Valley National Park Map; USGS Ubehebe Peak and Teakettle Junction quads

Trailhead facilities: The parking area is near the end of the dirt road.

Finding the trailhead: From Grapevine Junction, take Ubehebe Crater Road northwest for 5.5 miles to the end of the pavement and the sign for Racetrack Valley Road. Turn right (southwest) onto Racetrack Valley Road. Four-wheel drive is recommended, but under normal weather conditions is unnecessary. Racetrack Valley Road is severely washboarded, but contains no other obstacles as far as The Racetrack. Go south on Racetrack Valley Road for 19.6 miles to Teakettle Junction. Bear right (southwest), and continue for 2.2 miles to the right (west) turn to Ubehebe Lead Mine Road (signed). The dirt road leads 0.7 mile to a parking area at the mine site. GPS: N36 44.712'/W117 34.902'

The Hike

Ubehebe Mine has a lengthy history, beginning in 1875 when copper ore was found here. The copper mine was not fully developed until early in the twentieth century, but the profitable ore was soon depleted. In 1908, lead mining began at the site and continued until 1928. Ubehebe Mine had another renaissance in the 1940s as a zinc mine. Mining activity came to an end in 1951.

After all this mining it is not surprising to find a plethora of mining artifacts in the valley and in the hills above. A miner's house is still standing; its door and windows ajar, stripped of its plumbing (the range lies outside), it is a well-preserved remnant of its midcentury inhabitants. Remember that it may be unwise to enter deserted buildings due to deer mice and hantavirus.

In the wash above there are other traces of the crude dwellings of miners. Stacked stone walls are still in place. The men worked inside rock walls by day and slept in them at night. Rusty debris and small, level tent sites are scattered about. A squeaky bedspring (burned and rusted) lies amid the creosote bushes. This is an appropriate place to pause and contemplate the bustle of activity and spirit of optimism that must have prevailed in this mining valley in its various heydays.

Below the housing area sits the ore chute, with rail tracks still leading from a mine opening. The area looks like it was deserted only a year ago. The sagging old tram cable still hangs from the tower atop the hill to the valley floor at 0.4 mile. Unsecured mine openings dot the hillside. Although the National Park Service has not posted its usual warning signs, do not get close to mines. The tram should also be given a wide berth.

The hike up the trail to the overlook at 0.5 mile gives you a magnificent aerial view of the mine encampment and the rolling hills of the Last Chance Range. Mine openings proliferate like rodent burrows. The rust-colored rock and earth in piles at each opening gives the mining operations an eerie fresh appearance, as if the work here just stopped yesterday, instead of seventy or one hundred years ago. Numerous wooden posts mark the mountainside along the trail to designate claims of long-gone prospectors. Crossing carefully beneath the hilltop tram tower, you arrive at trail's end and a view westward of winding Corridor Canyon.

A hike down Corridor Canyon is a nice addition to the Ubehebe Lead Mine hike. From the mine chute, drop generally westward down the wide and graveled wash to the head of Corridor Canyon. At 0.3 mile, a tantalizing narrow stair-step chute of a canyon enters from the left (south), inviting exploration—although large boulders may prevent you from getting very far.

At about 1 mile, impressive cliff walls soar high to the left (south), whereas the right (north) side is marked by folded rock layers altered by fault lines. Below, as the canyon turns left (west), are colorful bands of rock. The cliffs are pockmarked with caverns and other small openings, some of which serve as active dens for animals.

The canyon is unique in that it provides both a closed-in experience, as well as far distant vistas of cliffs, overshadowed by even higher cliff layers beyond, opening to expansive views of adjacent and faraway mountains. Hike another 1.5 miles in the wide wash before turning around and retracing your steps. For more of the same you can continue down the wash for up to 2.5 additional miles, making for a pleasant day hike of up to 10 miles out and back.

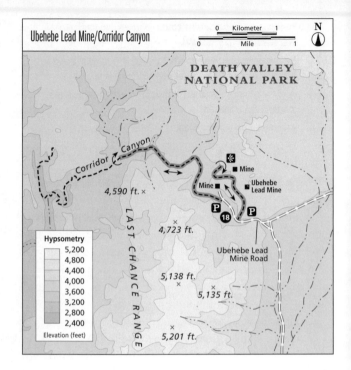

Ubehebe Lead Mine/Corridor Canyon

DEATH VALLEY NATIONAL PARK

Corridor Canyon

4,590 ft. ×

Mine ■
Mine ■ Ubehebe Lead Mine
■

P 18 P

× 4,723 ft.

Ubehebe Lead Mine Road

5,138 ft. ×

× 5,135 ft.

× 5,201 ft.

Hypsometry
5,200
4,800
4,400
4,000
3,600
3,200
2,800
2,400
Elevation (feet)

LAST CHANCE RANGE

Miles and Directions

Mine hike:

0.0 Back up the road from the miner's shack, on the north side by the low stone wall, the trail leads up the hillside.

0.4 Pass a tram cable tower at the hilltop.

0.5 Arrive at the scenic overlook.

1.0 Return to the trailhead by the same route.

Canyon hike:

0.0 Just beyond the mine chute, head west down the wash.

0.3 A chute canyon enters from the left (south).

1.0 Reach the dramatic cliffs; continue down the canyon until you decide to turn around.

2.5 By this point you've seen what makes this canyon special, but you can continue on for up to 2.5 more miles.

5.0 Anywhere along the route, turn around and retrace your steps to the trailhead.

10.0 Arrive back at the trailhead.

19 Ubehebe and Little Hebe Craters

These volcanic craters are a fascinating geology lesson on the forces that helped form Death Valley. A short loop hike around the large Ubehebe Crater and the several smaller ones allows you to witness the complex erosion patterns that have occurred since the craters' geologically recent birth.

Distance: 1.5-mile loop
Approximate hiking time: 1 to 2 hours
Elevation change: 320 feet
Difficulty: Easy; moderate to the bottom of the large crater
Trail surface: Volcanic cinder
Best season: Late October through April
Maps: Trails Illustrated Death Valley National Park Map; USGS Ubehebe Crater quad
Trailhead facilities: A signed parking area with interpretive signs is on the paved road.

Finding the trailhead: From the Grapevine Junction of Scotty's Castle Road and Ubehebe Crater Road, 45 miles north of Furnace Creek, take Ubehebe Crater Road northwest. Drive 5.7 miles to the parking area for the Ubehebe Crater/Little Hebe Crater trailhead. The parking area is on the eastern side of the one-way loop of paved road at the end of Ubehebe Crater Road. GPS: N37 0.504'/W117 28.391'

The Hike

The volcanic region at the north end of the Cottonwood Mountains, near Scotty's Castle, is evidence of recent cataclysmic events in Death Valley, geologically speaking. The huge Ubehebe Crater was created less than 1,000 years ago when magma heated groundwater and the pressure from the resulting steam blew the overlying rock away. This explosion covered 6 square miles of desert with volcanic debris 150 feet deep. Called a maar volcano by geologists, Ubehebe is a crater without a cone. The rim has been eroding ever since the explosion, gradually filling the crater with alluvial fans. Quite appropriately, the Shoshone Indians of Death Valley dubbed the crater "Basket in the Rock."

Little Hebe Crater, directly south, is much younger. Having exploded about 300 to 500 years ago, it is one of the newest geologic features of Death Valley. Little Hebe's rim is neat and well defined, exhibiting little of the erosion that has reduced Ubehebe's edge.

You can learn a lot about the craters by reading the information on the board and glancing at these monstrous holes in the earth. But there is no substitute for hiking all the way around this monumental display of volcanic power if you want to really appreciate the dimensions of the Ubehebe complex. Hold on to your hat, as this can be a very windy place.

The first quarter of the hike takes you along the rim of the main crater. The size of the hole is overpowering. It is almost a half mile from rim to rim. Alluvial fans have formed on the walls as the rains tear down the crater's edges.

In the vicinity of Ubehebe Crater, there are as many as twelve additional craters, all examples of more maar activity. You will see numerous craters in various stages of eroding deterioration. Little Hebe stands out as a jewel of a crater. Neat and trim, this volcanic chasm is only 200 yards across. The younger, fresher rim has barely begun to weather. Volcanic materials are very durable. Clearly visible on the walls of Little Hebe are the layers beneath the earth's surface. Especially noticeable is a thick layer of viscous lava that had oozed from the earth's interior prior to the explosion of Little Hebe.

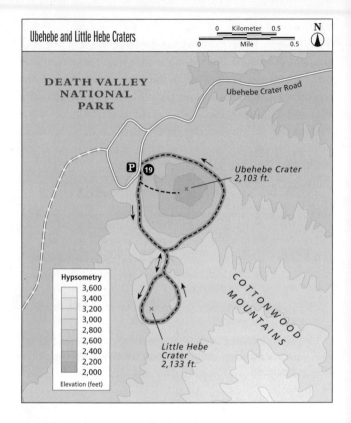

After the tour around Little Hebe at 0.7 mile, continue your hike around the main crater, which seems even larger after visiting its younger neighbor. A well-defined trail leads around Ubehebe, ending at 1.5 miles. The power of nature to modify the terrain via volcanic action stands in sharp contrast with the more gradual erosive forces that are demonstrated elsewhere in Death Valley. The earth has not finished rearranging its surface here—the forces that created Ubehebe and Little Hebe are merely dormant, not dead.

Option

The 0.3-mile trail into the crater slopes downward from the rim at 1.3 miles. The volcanic cinder trail descends nearly 450 vertical feet to the floor of the crater. After major rainstorms the crater also features a small lake. Most of the time it is dry. The climb back to the parking area requires some exertion due to the skidding quality of the volcanic cinders.

Miles and Directions

0.0 The trail goes south from the information board at the parking area.

0.3 The trail climbs; bear left at the Y intersection. The trail to the right has eroded on both sides and may be hazardous.

0.4 Reach a maze of use trails on the small plateau between the craters; a sign directs you south to Little Hebe Crater. Follow the trail around Little Hebe.

0.7 Back at the intersection continue to hike around the large Ubehebe Crater.

1.5 Return to the trailhead or take the optional trail to the bottom of the crater which adds about 0.6 mile to the overall distance.

20 Eureka Dunes

In a remote desert valley, against the dramatic backdrop of the colorful Last Chance Mountains, rise the Eureka Sand Dunes. They are the tallest sand dunes in California and the second highest in all of North America, although their constantly shifting nature would make that difficult to measure. These dunes are home to endemic plants and animals. Your cross-country walk to their summit will be a soft sandy stroll.

Distance: 3-mile loop
Approximate hiking time: 2 hours
Elevation change: 600 feet
Difficulty: Moderate due to a steep climb on soft sand
Trail surface: All-sand on a cross-country route
Best season: October into April

Maps: Trails Illustrated Death Valley National Park Map; USGS Last Chance Range quad
Trailhead facilities: You will find a parking area, monument, primitive campsites, picnic tables, and vault toilet at the end of the dirt road.

Finding the trailhead: From the south, take Scotty's Castle Road to Grapevine Junction and proceed northwest on Ubehebe Crater Road for 2.8 miles to Big Pine Road, also known as the North Entrance Highway and Death Valley Road. The turnoff is signed EUREKA DUNES 45 MILES. Turn north onto the washboard, graded gravel Big Pine Road and drive 34 miles to South Eureka Valley Road, the road to the Eureka Dunes. Turn left (south) onto this road and drive 10 miles to the end-of-the-road picnic/parking area near the northern base of the dunes. From the north, you can reach Eureka Dunes from Big Pine via 28 miles of paved road and 11 miles of graded dirt road. At South Eureka Valley Road, turn right (south) and follow the narrow road for the final 10 miles to the base of the dunes. GPS: N37 6.840'/W117 40.051'

The Hike

For those of us who never completely outgrew our love of sandboxes, this place is paradise. The Eureka Dunes, located within the expanded northern portion of the park, are a fascinating island of sand in a desert sea. From a distance, this 1- by 3-mile mountain of sand seems to hover over the remote Eureka Valley floor. Although not extensive, these dunes are the tallest in California and likely the tallest in North America. From the dry lakebed at their western edge, the Eureka Dunes rise abruptly more than 600 feet. Equally impressive are the sheer faces of the Last Chance Mountains to the immediate east, with their bands of pink, black, and gray limestone.

If the sand here is completely dry, you may hear one of the most unusual sounds in the desert: singing sand. When the sand cascades down the steepest pitch of the highest dune, a rumbling sound comparable to the bass note of a pipe organ emanates from it. No one knows exactly why this happens, but the friction of smooth-textured sand grains sliding against each other probably has something to do with it.

These dunes receive more moisture than others in the park because they are positioned at the western foot of a high mountain range that intercepts passing storms. The isolation of the Eureka Dunes, far from any other dunes, has resulted in endemic plant and animal species. For example, the entire range of five species of beetles and three plants is limited to these lofty mounds.

The three endemic plant species are shining locoweed, Eureka dune grass, and Eureka evening primrose, which are listed as endangered species under the federal Endangered

Species Act. Shining locoweed is a hummock-forming plant with root nodules that fix nitrogen from the air, a vital plant nutrient not available in the sand. When windblown sand covers the leafy flower shoots of the Eureka evening primrose, a new rosette of leaves forms at the tip. Large, white flowers bloom at night so that moths and other pollinators can avoid daytime heat. Usually, Eureka dune grass is the only plant on the higher slopes of the dunes. Its thick roots hold shifting sand, forming hummocks. Stiff, spiny leaf tips discourage herbivores.

The Eureka Dunes are a small, ecologically unique place requiring special care. Camp and keep vehicles a good distance from the base of the dunes, which is where most of the endemic plants and animals live. If possible, walk where others have in order to concentrate the impact away from pristine areas. You can help protect endangered species by not walking on these sensitive plant communities.

From the monument/parking/camping area, head east cross-country along the base of the dunes toward the color-banded Last Chance Mountains that rise an impressive 4,000 feet above the Eureka Valley floor. Hiking along the base provides a constantly changing perspective of this unusual landscape, as well as a good warm-up for climbing the steep backside of the dunes. A profusion of animal tracks will appear, as will the circular paths of grass tips etched in the sand by the ever-changing wind.

At 0.8 mile, the initial flat stretch becomes laced with gullies strewn with volcanic "bombs" embedded in the sand. At this point, begin curving around the base of the dunes to the right (south). This wonderfully wide-open trek stands in startling contrast to the closed-in feeling one gets when exploring the deep canyons of Death Valley.

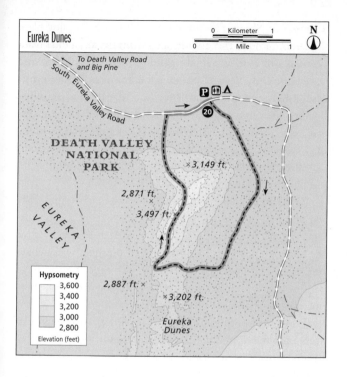

At about 1.5 miles, begin climbing westward up any one of the several narrow knife-edge sand ridges that converge at the apex of the dunes. A vertical gain of about 600 feet to the 3,497-foot apex is spread over about 0.7 mile, with most of the climb during the final 0.2 mile. The dry lakebed, expansive Eureka Valley, colorful Last Chance range, and the dunes themselves combine to form a stunning 360-degree panorama. To complete the 3-mile loop, continue back down along narrow ridges and steep scooped-out bowls of sand in a north to northwesterly direction to the trailhead.

Option

Another choice for climbing the dunes, which can be hard work at times in the loose, shifting sand, is a shorter out-and-back route. This more direct approach to the 600-foot climb is a 1.5-mile round-trip hike by way of a series of knife ridges. Because of the long driving distance to the trailhead, the longer 3-mile loop may be your better choice. In so choosing, you'll gain more intimacy with the dunes and their majestic Last Chance Mountains backdrop.

Miles and Directions

0.0 Begin from either the picnic tables on the north or the monument in the parking area.

1.5 Begin climbing around the east side of the dunes.

2.2 Reach the top of the dunes.

3.0 Complete the loop back to the trailhead.

Day Hiker Checklist

Use the following checklist as you assemble your gear for day hiking in Death Valley National Park:

- ❏ sturdy, well-broken-in, light-to-medium weight hiking boots
- ❏ broad-brimmed hat, which must be wiproof
- ❏ long-sleeved shirt for sun protection
- ❏ long pants for protection against sun and brush
- ❏ water; two quarts to one gallon/day (depending on season), in sturdy screw-top plastic containers
- ❏ large-scale topographic map (quad) and GPS
- ❏ whistle, mirror, and matches (for emergency signals)
- ❏ flashlight (in case your hike takes longer than you expect)
- ❏ sunblock and lip sunscreen
- ❏ insect repellent (in season)
- ❏ pocketknife
- ❏ small first-aid kit: tweezers, bandages, antiseptic, moleskin, snakebite extractor kit
- ❏ bee sting kit (over the counter antihistamine or epinephrine by prescription) as needed for the season
- ❏ windbreaker (or rain gear in season)
- ❏ lunch or snack, with plastic bag for your trash
- ❏ toilet paper, with a plastic zipper bag to pack it out
- ❏ your FalconGuide

Optional gear:

- ❏ camera
- ❏ binoculars
- ❏ bird and plant guidebooks
- ❏ notebook and pen/pencil
- ❏ trekking poles